RAND M^cNALLY

Atlas of
American
History

Project Manager
Carole Wicklander

Book Production Editor
Louise Frederiksen

Map Production Editor
Charles J. MacDonald

Managing Editor
Margaret McNamara

Digital Cartographers
Barbara Benstead-Strassheim
Elizabeth A. Hunt
Amy L. Troesch

Digital Cartography Project Manager
Thomas Vitacco

Cartographic Editorial
Robert K. Argersinger
Gregory P. Babiak
Jill M. Stift

Cartographic Production
Norma Denny
Jim Purvis

Manual Cartography Project Manager
David Zapenski

Designer
Donna McGrath

Production Manager
Robert Sanders

Typesetting
Yvonne Rosenberg

Photo Credit
Images provided by ©1999 PhotoDisc, Inc.

Printed in the United States of America

Rand McNally & Company
Skokie, Illinois 60076-8906

  3456789-RM-03-02-01-00-99

ISBN #528-84500-4

For information about ordering *Atlas of American History*, call 1-800-678-7263, or visit our website at www.k12online.com.

Table of Contents

Introducing Atlas of American History

The features of *Atlas of American History* described below enhance understanding of America's past. They support and extend information from textbooks and primary sources. They provide additional links between history and geography.

Features of *Atlas of American History*

▲ Historical Maps

Maps are arranged chronologically. Each map includes a title that describes its content and dates that indicate the period of history it shows. Compare maps of the same area in different time periods to view historical changes.

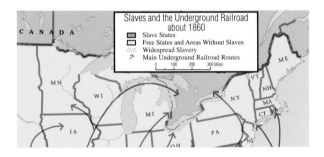

▲ Map Legends and Labels

A map legend explains the colors and symbols used on a map. Historical maps often use solid or dashed lines to indicate routes of explorers or other groups of people. These routes may be labeled on the map. Labels also identify sites of historical events.

Captions

Each map has a caption that helps explain the content of the map. It may provide information about the historical context of the map or point out an important feature of the map. Legends, labels, and captions help tell the story of American history.

Population by National Origin, 1790

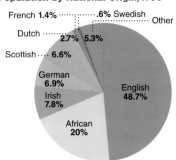

◄ Graphs

Some graphs in *Atlas of American History* illustrate information from the maps. Others provide additional information about American history. They may compare data or show changes over time.

Populations of United States Colonies and States, 1650-1990

States	1650	1700	1750	1770
Alabama				
Alaska				
Arizona				
Arkansas				
California				
Colorado				
Connecticut	4,139	25,970	111,280	183,881
Delaware	185	2,470	28,704	35,496

▲ Databank

The databank is a reference section on pages 72-75 of the atlas. It provides tables of information about the United States and its people.

1776	
People	Juan Bautista de Anza establishes a presidio at San Francisco.

1776	
Events	Declaration of Independence is signed in Philadelphia.

1776	
Literature	*"To His Excellency, General Washington,"* by a slave named Phillis Wheatley, is printed in the Pennsylvania Magazine.

◄ Chronologies

Each section of *Atlas of American History* includes a chronology. It lists people, events, and literature associated with the time period represented on the maps in that section. These listings provide connections that aid understanding of history.

◄ Index

The index is an alphabetical listing of the places and topics included in *Atlas of American History*. The index shows the page number(s) on which each entry appears. It provides explanatory information about many entries and refers to related entries when appropriate.

Periods of American History

Historians may divide American history into time periods in many different ways. Some periods may center around a theme, such as exploration. Others may center around an important event, such as the American Revolution.

Rand McNally *Atlas of American History* is divided into sections based on time periods described below. Some periods overlap to provide coverage of political and social history. Maps are organized chronologically within each section.

1. Beginnings (prehistory-1620)

Thousands of years ago, hunters from Asia migrated to the lands now called the Americas. These people, now referred to as American Indians or Native Americans, settled throughout the continents. They developed many different cultures, depending upon the environments in which they lived. They remained the only people in the Western Hemisphere until about A.D. 1000, when Vikings from Norway migrated to the coast of North America.

During the 1400s, European demand for Asian goods led Columbus to sail west across the Atlantic Ocean in search of a route to Asia. His discovery of a world previously unknown to Europeans touched off an age of exploration. During the 1500s, Europeans explored and claimed land in the Americas.

2. Establishing Colonies (1600-1775)

During the 1600s and early 1700s, Europeans came to the Americas for many different reasons. English settlers came seeking the freedom to wor-ship as they pleased. Spaniards came to find gold and to spread Christianity. French trappers came to establish fur trade. Dutch settlers came for the promise of land. In addition, many Africans were brought to the Americas as slaves.

By the mid-1700s, English claims extended along the Atlantic coast, and the French controlled the vast interior of North America. Britain and France competed for control of the continent. As a result of the French and Indian War (1754-1763), Britain gained Canada and all of North America east of the Mississippi River.

3. Forming a New Nation (1775-1800)

English settlers in North America developed a prosperous economy and a way of life that differed from that in Great Britain. They began to resent Britain's control. They declared their independence and fought a revolution to win their freedom. As a result, the United States became an independent nation.

The original thirteen states stretched along the Atlantic coast. The western boundary of the new nation extended to the Mississippi River. Americans began to settle lands west of the Appalachian Mountains. The national government passed laws providing for the sale of western lands and the addition of new states.

4. The Nation Expands and Changes (1790-1870)

Much of the history of the United States is a story of westward movement. Between 1803 and 1848, the nation expanded its boundaries from the Mississippi River to the Pacific Coast. Pioneers had settled most of the land east of the Mississippi River by 1840.

People	**1769** Junípero Serra starts first Spanish mission in what is now California.	**1804** Meriwether Lewis and William Clark lead expedition from St. Louis to the Pacific Ocean.	**1933** President Franklin Roosevelt creates TVA to develop the natural resources of the Tennessee Valley.
Events	**about 700 B.C.** The Adena (early North American Indians) build mounds in what is now Ohio.	**1565** Spaniards establish St. Augustine, FL, first permanent European settlement in what is now the United States.	**1787** Founders write the U.S. Constitution in Philadelphia, PA.
Literature	**1608** *A True Relation of Occurrences in Virginia*, by John Smith, describes the founding of Jamestown.	**1704** Sarah Kemble Knight's *Journal* describes the author's horseback journey from Boston to New York.	**1868** *Little Women*, by Louisa May Alcott, tells the story of four sisters growing up in New England in the mid-1800s.

In the early 1800s, fur trappers, traders, and miners pushed west of the Mississippi River, seeking economic opportunities. Soon they were followed by farmers and ranchers who settled the land. The promise of land and the hope of a better life also attracted millions of European immigrants to the United States.

5. A Nation Divided (1850-1865)

Different ways of life developed in the North and the South. Southern agriculture was based on slave labor. Industrial states in the North outlawed slavery. As settlers moved westward, new states were created. The question of whether to allow slavery in the new states led to conflict between the North and the South.

Debate and compromise failed to solve the problems. Eleven southern states withdrew from the Union. Between 1861 and 1865, the North and the South fought against each other in the Civil War.

6. Emerging as a Modern Nation (1860-1920)

Within 25 years after the Civil War ended, the process of settling the United States from coast to coast was completed. The settlement of the West also brought an end to the Native American way of life. The federal government sent soldiers to stop uprisings and move Indians onto reservations.

As the United States became an industrial nation, people moved to cities to work in factories. Millions of European immigrants also came to the United States seeking jobs.

The nation acquired territories overseas and began to emerge as a modern nation. By fighting in World War I, the United States also proved that it had become a world power.

7. Challenges and Changes in the 20th Century (1920-1990)

A period of prosperity followed World War I. However, the stock market crash in 1929 plunged the nation into an economic depression that lasted throughout the 1930s. During those years, the actions of powerful dictators in Europe led to World War II.

The United States fought in World War II from 1941 to 1945. It emerged as the leader of the free world, and the Soviet Union emerged as the leader of the Communist world. During the following decades, the United States intervened in many parts of the world to stop the spread of Communism.

8. Entering a New Millennium (1990 and beyond)

The United States has compiled information about the American population every ten years since 1790, when the first census was taken. According to the 1990 census, more than three-fourths of the country's 250 million people lived in cities. Americans born in 1990 could expect to live longer than any previous generation. Although many Americans lived in poverty in 1990, the United States had one of the world's highest standards of living.

The United States faces many challenges as it enters a new millennium. It must meet the needs of its diverse population. It must also continue its role of leadership in a rapidly changing world. The story of America is ongoing because today's events will become tomorrow's history.

1955
Rosa Parks protests segregation in Montgomery, AL by refusing to give up bus seat to white passenger.

1969
U.S. astronaut Neil Armstrong becomes first person to walk on the moon.

1989
Colin Powell, son of Jamaican immigrants, becomes first African American to head Joint Chiefs of Staff.

1848
Discovery of gold in California brings settlers to the West.

1941
Japanese bombing of Pearl Harbor, Hawaii, brings U.S. into World War II.

1970
Americans participate in Earth Day, a nationwide demonstration of concern for the environment.

1932
Little House in the Big Woods, by Laura Ingalls Wilder, describes life in the Midwest in the 1870s and 1880s.

1976
Roots: The Saga of an American Family, by Alex Haley, traces the author's ancestry back to the African slave trade.

1989
The Joy Luck Club, by Amy Tan, tells the experiences of Chinese women in San Francisco after World War II.

Benefits of Using Rand McNally *Atlas of American History*

Events gain fuller meaning.

Knowing where events took place gives them fuller meaning and often explains causes and effects. For example, the map of the final campaign of the American Revolution, on page 27, shows how American and French forces trapped the British at Yorktown. It helps explain why Cornwallis surrendered.

Connections among events are clarified.

Through the visual power of historical maps, the links between and among events become clear. The maps on pages 12 and 13 show international trade routes, 1350-1450, and Portuguese routes to India in the 1400s. They help explain why Europeans wanted to find an all-water route to Asia. They provide the background to understanding the age of exploration that followed Columbus's discovery of the Americas.

Similarities and differences become apparent.

The maps in *Atlas of American History* provide an opportunity to compare and contrast places over time. Compare the map of North America in 1763, on page 23, with the map of North America in 1783 on page 28. These maps show the emergence of the United States on a continent claimed by Britain and Spain.

The maps in this atlas also provide an opportunity to compare and contrast regions of the United States. The map titled "A Quarreling People," on page 41, indicates differences between the North and the South at the time of the Civil War.

The influence of sense of place is conveyed.

Maps in *Atlas of American History* convey people's sense of place at a particular time in history. The map titled "Opportunities and Uncertainties," on page 58, is a good example. The map's polar projection emphasizes how near the Soviet Union is to the United States. It reflects Americans' fear of nuclear attack from the north during the postwar period of tension between the United States and the Soviet Union.

Trends emerge.

The maps in this atlas show trends in American history. The map of Westward Expansion, on pages 36-37, shows the sequence in which the United States acquired land. It indicates the westward movement of settlement patterns. The maps on pages 38, 48, and 61 indicate changing trends in immigration.

The story of American history is communicated.

The text in *Atlas of American History* presents a chronological overview of American history and summarizes key events. It provides cross curricular connections by listing literature that clarifies or expands historical understandings. It highlights people whose accomplishments reflect American ideals.

The *Did You Know?* feature on each section opening page provides an interesting sidelight to history. Like the example below, each of these features demonstrates how history has influenced the American experience.

A picture of the Greek god Atlas, supporting the earth on his shoulders, appeared on the title page of an early book of maps. Later, people began to call a collection of maps an *atlas*.

Section 1   (Prehistory-1620)

Beginnings

To learn about **prehistory**, or the time before human beings learned to write, scientists study the physical evidence that early people left behind. This evidence suggests the first Americans migrated from Asia between 25,000 and 8,000 years ago. The descendants of these people, now called Native Americans or American Indians, spread throughout the Americas and developed different cultures.

Historical evidence indicates that Vikings from Norway established a settlement in North America about A.D. 1000. During the 1400s, increased demand for Asian goods led European nations to seek a water route to Asia. Columbus was attempting to achieve this goal when he discovered a world previously unknown to Europeans.

During the 1500s, European explorers who came to the Americas found continents inhabited by native peoples of diverse cultures, from hunters and gatherers to advanced civilizations. Although figures vary greatly, the graph at the right indicates estimates of Native American populations around that time.

◀ The Cliff Palace in Mesa Verde, Colorado, was built by the Anasazi around 1100.

In 1524 Verrazano, ▶ sailing for France, explored the Atlantic coast of what is now North Carolina.

Did You Know ?

Scientists discovered a spearhead among bones of ancient bison near Folsom, New Mexico. These animals became extinct about 10,000 years ago. This discovery proved people had migrated to the region by about 8000 B.C.

Estimates of Native American Populations in 1492

Region	Population in millions
North America	~4.5
Mexico	~21.5
Central America	~5
Caribbean	~6
Andes	~11
Lowland South America	~9

(Axis: 0, 5, 10, 15, 20, 25 — Population in millions)

	about A.D. 1000	**1492**	**1587**
People	Leif Ericson establishes a Viking settlement on the east coast of North America.	Christopher Columbus lands on San Salvador.	Virginia Dare, first English child born in America, is born on Roanoke Island.
	about 23,000 B.C.	**1325**	**about 1570**
Events	First Americans probably migrate from Asia to North America.	Aztecs build Tenochtitlán on site of present-day Mexico City.	Five Indian tribes in what is now New York form League of the Iroquois.
	1298	**1504**	**1552**
Literature	*Description of the World*, by Marco Polo, tells of the Italian trader's journey from Venice to China.	*New World*, a letter by Amerigo Vespucci, becomes the basis for naming America.	*In Defense of the Indian*, by Bartolomé de Las Casas, criticizes the Spanish for abusing Indians on Hispaniola.

During the Ice Ages, much of Earth's water was frozen in glaciers. These huge ice sheets covered much of what is now Canada and the northern United States. Scientists believe a land bridge existed where the Bering Strait now separates Asia and Alaska. Between 25,000 and 10,000 years ago, people from Asia may have migrated across the land bridge and spread throughout North America and South America.

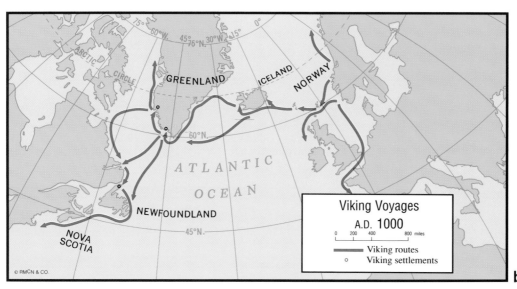

About A.D. 1000, Norwegian Vikings, who had settled in Greenland, explored the coast of North America. They established a settlement in what is now Newfoundland, Canada.

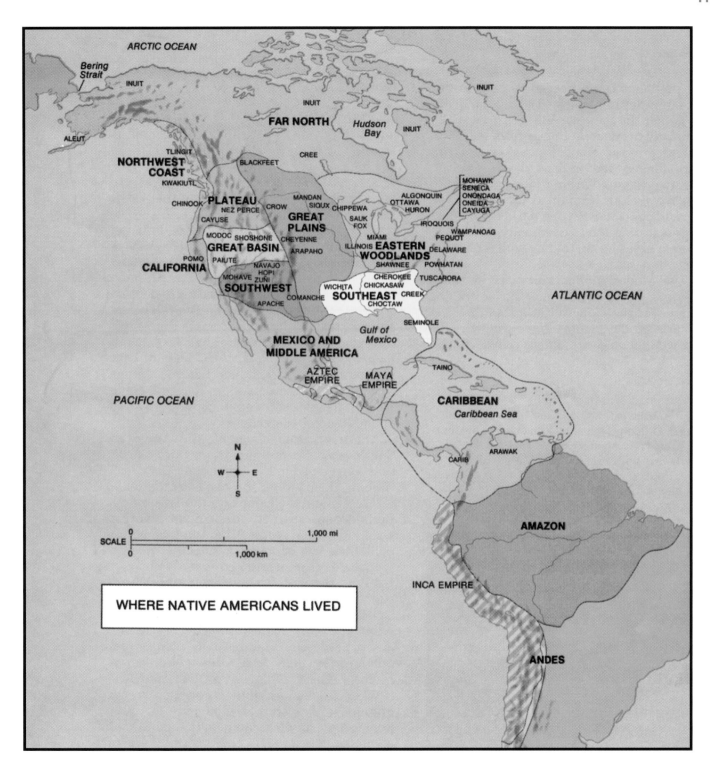

Environments in which tribes of Native Americans or American Indians followed a similar way of life are called culture areas. The culture areas shown on the map existed around 1500, when Europeans began to arrive in the Americas. The map also lists major tribes of Native Americans within each culture area.

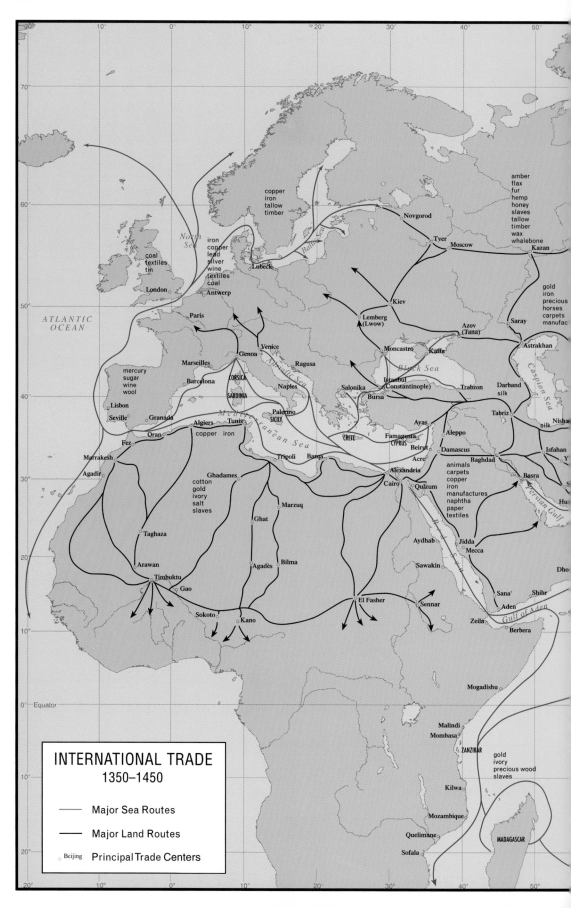

amber
flax
fur
hemp
honey
slaves
tallow
timber
wax
whalebone

copper
iron
tallow
timber

Novgorod

Tver

Moscow

Kazan

North Sea

iron
copper
lead
silver
wine
textiles
coal

Lubeck

Kiev

gold
iron
precious
horses
carpets
manufac

coal
textiles
tin

London

Antwerp

Lemberg
(Lwow)

Saray

Azov
(Tana)

Astrakhan

ATLANTIC OCEAN

Paris

Venice

Moncastro

Kaffa

Black Sea

Caspian Sea

Genoa

Ragusa

Marseilles

Istanbul
(Constantinople)

Trabzon

Darband
silk

mercury
sugar
wine
wool

Barcelona

CORSICA

Naples

Salonika

Bursa

Tabriz

Nisha

SARDINIA

Palermo

silk

Lisbon

SICILY

Ayas

Aleppo

Isfahan

Seville

Granada

Mediterranean Sea

Famagusta
CYPRUS

Damascus

Y

Algiers

Tunis

CRETE

Beirut

Baghdad

Basra

Isfahan

Fez

Oran

copper   iron

Acre

animals
carpets
copper
iron
manufactures
naphtha
paper
textiles

Marrakesh

Tripoli

Barqa

Alexandria

Hu

Agadir

Ghadames

Cairo

Quizum

S

cotton
gold
ivory
salt
slaves

Marzuq

Persian Gulf

Taghaza

Ghat

Aydhab

Jidda
Mecca

Dho

Arawan

Agadès

Bilma

Sawakin

Sana'

Shihr

Timbuktu

Gao

Sennar

Aden

Gulf of Aden

Sokoto

Kano

El Fasher

Zeila

Berbera

Equator

Mogadishu

Malindi

Mombasa

ZANZIBAR

gold
ivory
precious wood
slaves

Kilwa

Mozambique

Quelimane

MADAGASCAR

Sofala

INTERNATIONAL TRADE
1350–1450

——— Major Sea Routes

▬▬▬ Major Land Routes

○ Beijing Principal Trade Centers

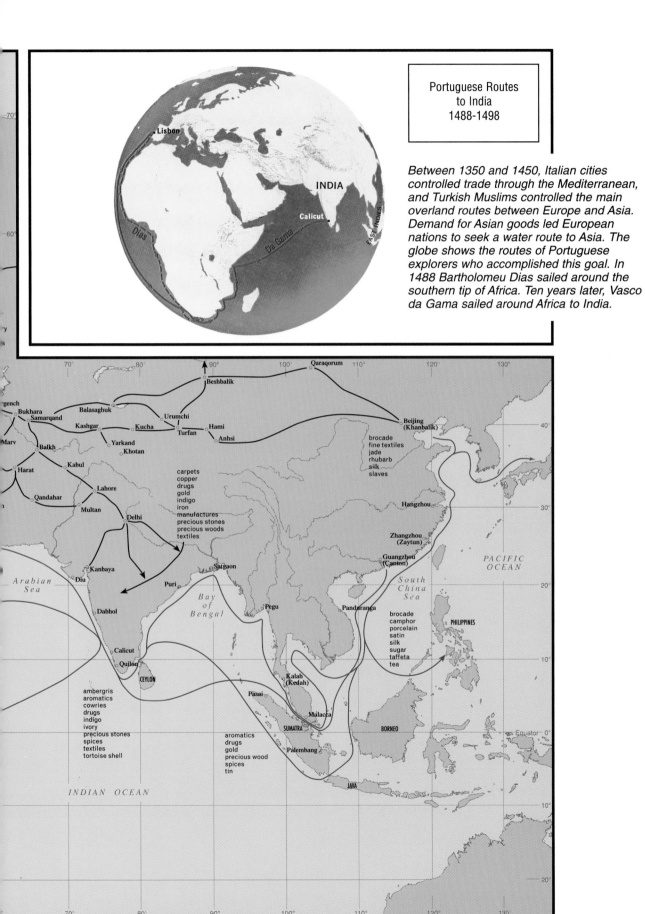

Portuguese Routes to India 1488-1498

Between 1350 and 1450, Italian cities controlled trade through the Mediterranean, and Turkish Muslims controlled the main overland routes between Europe and Asia. Demand for Asian goods led European nations to seek a water route to Asia. The globe shows the routes of Portuguese explorers who accomplished this goal. In 1488 Bartholomeu Dias sailed around the southern tip of Africa. Ten years later, Vasco da Gama sailed around Africa to India.

Lisbon

INDIA

Calicut

EAST INDIES

Dias

Da Gama

Qaraqorum
Beshbalik
Urgench
Bukhara
Samarqand
Balasaghuk
Urumchi
Kashgar
Kucha
Hami
Marv
Balkh
Yarkand
Turfan
Anhsi
Khotan
Harat
Kabul
Beijing
(Khanbalik)

brocade
fine textiles
jade
rhubarb
silk
slaves

Qandahar
Lahore
Multan
Delhi

carpets
copper
drugs
gold
indigo
iron
manufactures
precious stones
precious woods
textiles

Hangzhou

Zhangzhou
(Zaytun)

Guangzhou
(Canton)

PACIFIC
OCEAN

Kanbaya
Diu
Satgaon
Puri
Arabian
Sea

Bay
of
Bengal

Pegu
Panduranga

South
China
Sea

brocade
camphor
porcelain
satin
silk
sugar
taffeta
tea

PHILIPPINES

Dabhol
Calicut
Quilon
CEYLON

Kalah
(Kedah)
Pasai

ambergris
aromatics
cowries
drugs
indigo
ivory
precious stones
spices
textiles
tortoise shell

aromatics
drugs
gold
precious wood
spices
tin

Malacca
SUMATRA
Palembang
BORNEO
Equator

JAVA

INDIAN OCEAN

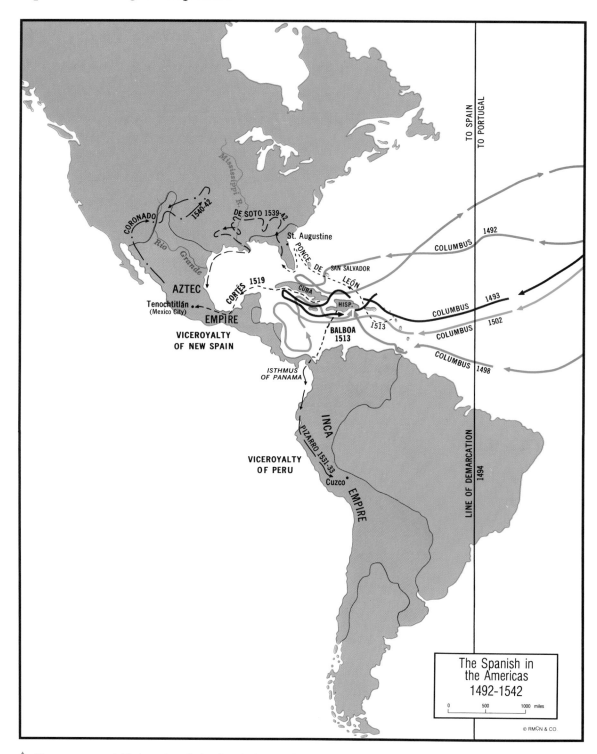

TO SPAIN
TO PORTUGAL

CORONADO
1540-42
DE SOTO 1539-42
Mississippi R.
St. Augustine
PONCE DE
SAN SALVADOR
LEÓN
1492
COLUMBUS
CORTÉS 1519
CUBA
AZTEC
HISP.
COLUMBUS 1493
Tenochtitlán
(Mexico City)
1513
COLUMBUS 1502
EMPIRE
BALBOA
VICEROYALTY
1513
COLUMBUS
OF NEW SPAIN
1498
Rio Grande

ISTHMUS
OF PANAMA

INCA
VICEROYALTY
PIZARRO 1531-33
OF PERU
Cuzco
EMPIRE

LINE OF DEMARCATION
1494

| The Spanish in |
| the Americas |
| 1492-1542 |

0   500   1000 miles

© RMCN & CO.

▲ *The voyages of Christopher Columbus led other Europeans to explore the Americas.*
Pope Alexander VI established the Line of Demarcation to prevent disputes between
Spain and Portugal over lands their explorers claimed. The Spanish conquered
Indian empires in Mexico and Peru.

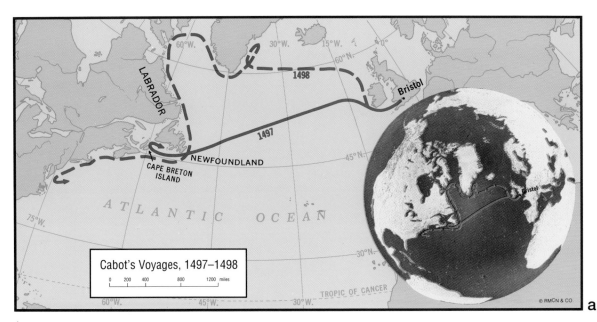

▲ John Cabot attempted to reach Asia by a northwest route across the Atlantic
Ocean. In 1497 and 1498, Cabot explored the coasts of present-day Labrador,
Newfoundland, and Cape Breton Island (Nova Scotia). His voyages gave
England a claim to North America.

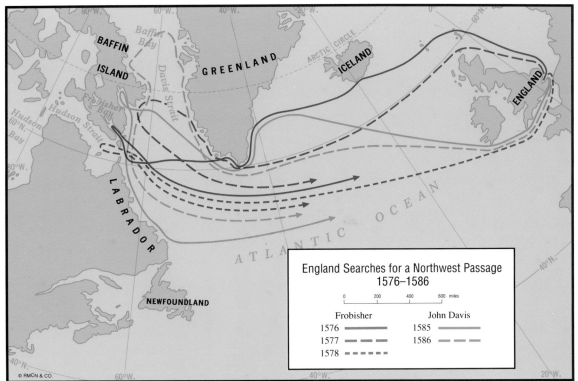

▲ In the 1570s and 1580s, England renewed its search for a water route to Asia
through North America. Martin Frobisher and John Davis explored the Atlantic
coast of what is now Canada and the area between Greenland and Baffin Island.

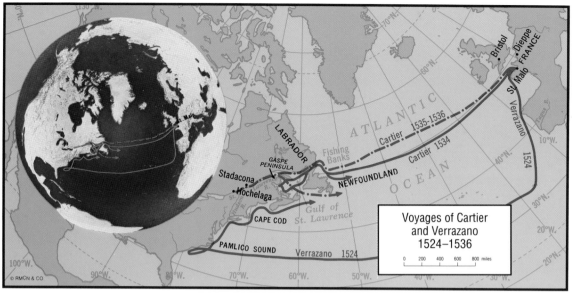

▲ France also sent explorers in search of a water route through North America. Giovanni da Verrazano explored the Atlantic coast from what is now North Carolina to Newfoundland. Jacques Cartier explored the St. Lawrence River and claimed the region for France.

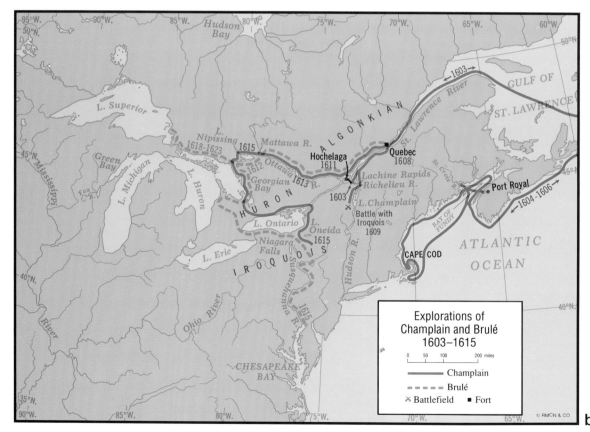

▲ Samuel de Champlain extended French claims in North America. In 1608 he founded the city of Quebec. He then helped the Algonquin and Huron Indians defeat the Iroquois. Etienne Brulé lived among the Huron Indians and explored the river systems of northeastern North America for France.

Section 2   *(1600-1775)*

Establishing Colonies

Between 1600 and 1775, Europeans established **colonies**, or settlements ruled by their homelands, in North America. The English settled along the Atlantic coast and eventually took over Dutch and Swedish colonies established there. By 1732 thirteen English colonies stretched along the east coast of the present United States from New Hampshire to Georgia.

The French claimed the vast interior of North America. English attempts to settle west of the Appalachians led to conflict between France and Britain. The French and Indian War gave Britain control of all land east of the Mississippi River.

The colonial population grew rapidly due to a high birth rate and increased immigration. People came to America seeking religious freedom and economic opportunities. Slave traders also brought thousands of unwilling immigrants from Africa.

◄ This stone canopy stands near the Massachusetts shore. It covers Plymouth Rock, which marks the spot near which the Pilgrims are believed to have stepped ashore.

Reproductions of ships that brought the first settlers to Jamestown are on the James River in Virginia. They are near the site of the first permanent English settlement in America. ►

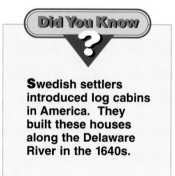

Growth of Colonial Population

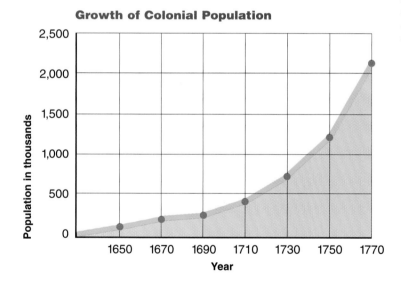

Population in thousands (y-axis: 0, 500, 1,000, 1,500, 2,000, 2,500)

Year (x-axis: 1650, 1670, 1690, 1710, 1730, 1750, 1770)

Did You Know?

Swedish settlers introduced log cabins in America. They built these houses along the Delaware River in the 1640s.

	1614		1626		1682
People	Pocahontas, daughter of Chief Powhatan, marries Jamestown colonist John Rolfe.		Peter Minuit purchases Manhattan Island from local Indians.		LaSalle claims Mississippi River Valley for France.

	1607		1620		1754
Events	Jamestown is founded.		Pilgrims settle Plymouth Colony.		French and Indian War begins at Fort Necessity.

	1640		1650		1733
Literature	The *Bay Psalm Book* is the first book written and published in the American colonies.		*The Tenth Muse Lately Sprung Up in America*, by Anne Bradstreet, describes home life in colonial New England.		*Poor Richard's Almanac*, by Ben Franklin, is published in Philadelphia.

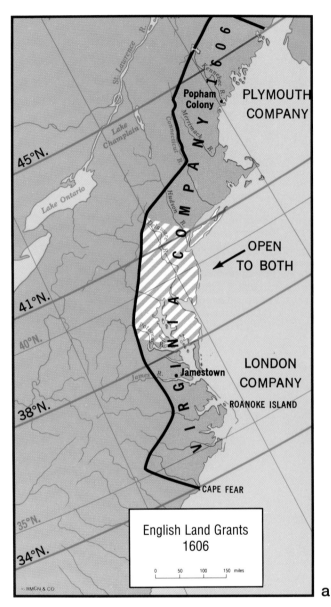

English Land Grants 1606

0   50   100   150 miles

a

▲ *The Plymouth Company and the London Company were groups of stockholders within the Virginia Company. Each group obtained a land grant from the English king to establish a colony in America. Land between 38° and 41° north latitude was open to both groups. Neither group was allowed to settle within 100 miles of the other.*

The Dutch bought Manhattan Island from Native Americans and established a trading center called New Amsterdam. They established other settlements along the Hudson River and later took over Swedish settlements along the Delaware River.
▼

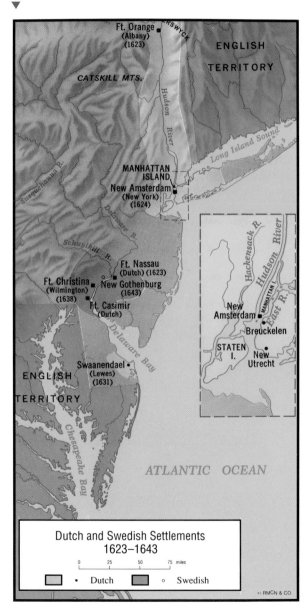

Dutch and Swedish Settlements 1623–1643

0   25   50   75 miles

◾ • Dutch   ◾ ○ Swedish

b

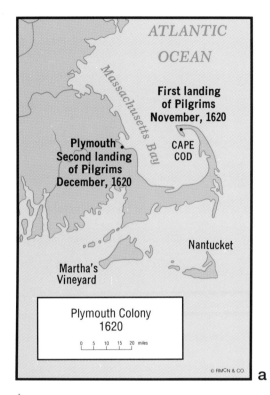

The Pilgrims named their colony Plymouth, after the English port from which they had sailed.

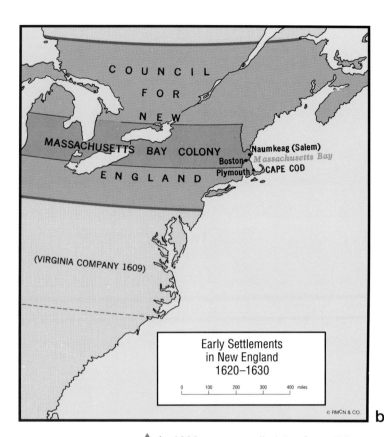

In 1620 a group called the Council for New England received a land grant from the English king. The Massachusetts Bay Colony was established on this land in 1628.

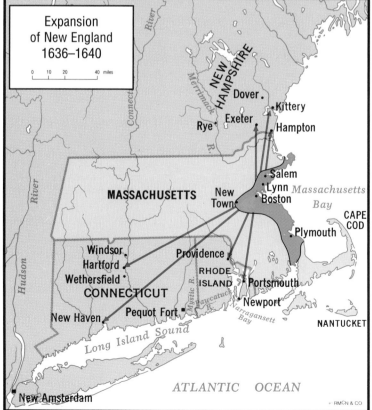

The Puritans established settlements in the eastern part of Massachusetts, shown in blue on the map. Plymouth became part of the Massachusetts Colony. People who disagreed with Puritan views left Massachusetts and established new colonies.

HUDSON'S   BAY   COMPANY

L. Superior

Quebec

Ft. Sault
Ste Marie   L. Nipissing   Ottawa   Montreal

JOLIET   R.

Ft. Michilimackinac   St. Lawrence R.

Ft. La
Présentation   JOLIET   Ft.
Crown
Point

Fort Frontenac
1673   Lake
Champlain

Wisconsin R.

Green
Bay   L. Huron   LA SALLE   L. Ontario

MARQUETTE-JOLIET   Fox R.   Ft. Rouillé   Ft. Oswego

LA SALLE   JOLIET   Ft. Niagara   IROQUOIS

Mississippi R.   L. Michigan

Ft. Pontchartrain
(Detroit)   Ft. Presqu'Isle
Ft. Le Boeuf
Ft. Venango

Ft. des
Miamis   St. Joseph R.   L. Erie   LA SALLE

R.   Ft. Sandusky

Illinois   Ft. Duquesne

Monongahela R.   Ft. Necessity

Ft. Crèvecoeur
1680

Missouri R.   Ft. Vincennes   Ohio R.   LA SALLE   ENGLISH

MARQUETTE-JOLIET   Kaskaskia

S H A W N E E

Arkansas R.   CHEROKEE

CHICKASAW   C R E E K S   Ft. Loudon

Ft. Prince George   ATLANTIC OCEAN

Point reached
1673

Red R.   Mississippi R.   LA SALLE   Alabama R.   Ft. Toulouse

French Influence
in North America
1682

■ French   □ English

0   50   100   200 miles

. Natchez

Biloxi .

. New Orleans   S P A N I S H

Cross erected
1682

G U L F   O F   M E X I C O

© RMCN & CO

▲ *France claimed the vast interior of North America, but it had little control over
the region because of a lack of settlers.*

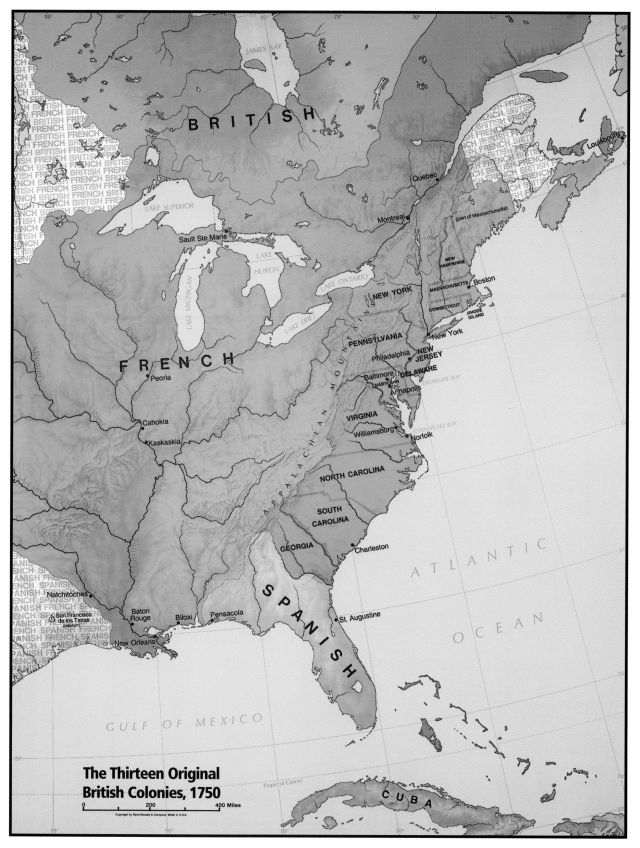

The Thirteen Original British Colonies, 1750

0   200   400 Miles

Copyright by Rand McNally & Company. Made in U.S.A.

BRITISH

FRENCH

SPANISH

JAMES BAY

Louisbourg

Quebec

LAKE SUPERIOR

Montreal

(part of Massachusetts)

Sault Ste Marie

NEW HAMPSHIRE

LAKE HURON

LAKE ONTARIO

LAKE ERIE

MASSACHUSETTS   Boston

NEW YORK

CONNECTICUT

RHODE ISLAND

New York

PENNSYLVANIA

NEW JERSEY

Philadelphia

DELAWARE

Peoria

Baltimore

MARYLAND

DELAWARE BAY

Annapolis

VIRGINIA

Cahokia

Williamsburg   Norfolk

CHESAPEAKE BAY

Kaskaskia

NORTH CAROLINA

SOUTH CAROLINA

GEORGIA

Charleston

ATLANTIC

Natchitoches

OCEAN

San Francisco de los Texas (mission)

Baton Rouge   Biloxi   Pensacola

St. Augustine

New Orleans

GULF OF MEXICO

Tropic of Cancer

CUBA

▲ *In about 150 years, the British established the 13 colonies that would become the United States. By 1750 the British colonies had a population of more than 1 million.*

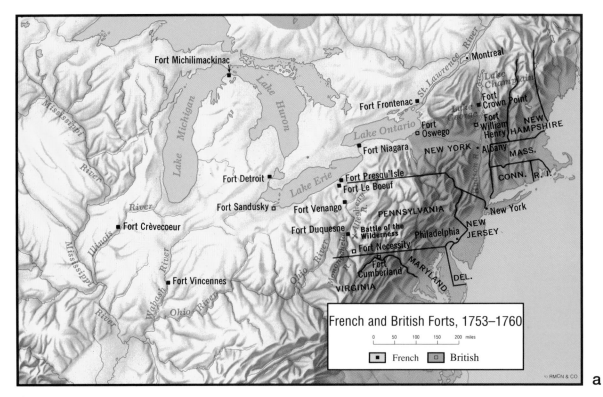

▲ *To keep the British east of the Appalachians, the French built a string of forts from Lake Erie to the Ohio River.*

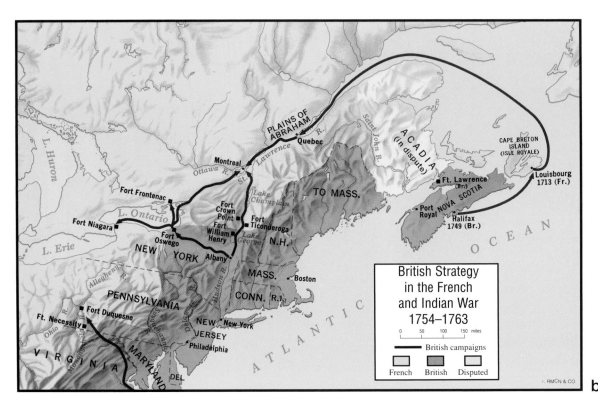

▲ *The British captured French forts in the St. Lawrence Valley and the eastern Great Lakes region.*

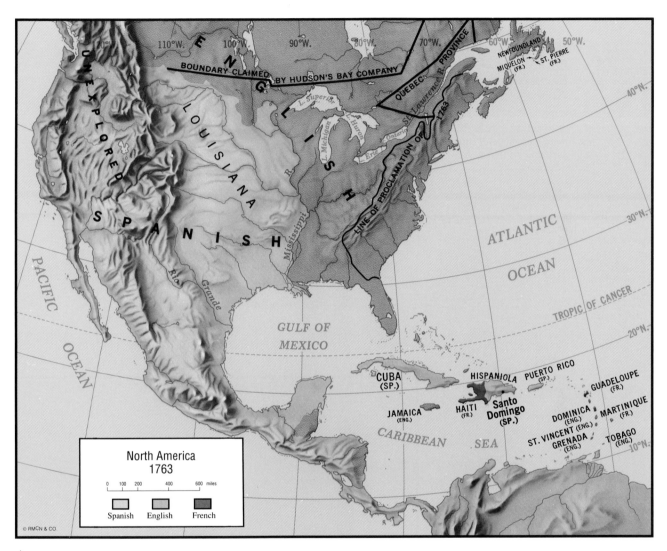

North America
1763

0   100   200   400   600 miles

Spanish   English   French

© RMCN & CO.

▲ The French and Indian War ended French control in North America. According to the Treaty of Paris in 1763, France kept only a few islands in the Caribbean. Britain acquired Canada and all French lands east of the Mississippi River. From Spain, France's ally in the war, Britain acquired Florida. To make up for the loss of Florida, France gave Spain the vast land between the Mississippi River and the Rocky Mountains.

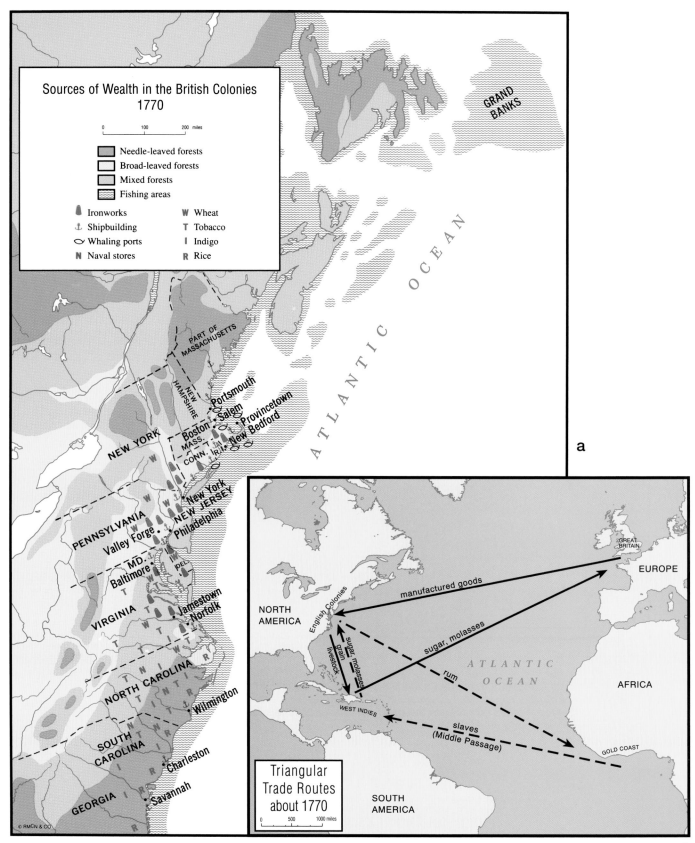

Sources of Wealth in the British Colonies 1770

0   100   200 miles

- Needle-leaved forests
- Broad-leaved forests
- Mixed forests
- Fishing areas

- Ironworks
- Shipbuilding
- Whaling ports
- Naval stores
- **W** Wheat
- **T** Tobacco
- **I** Indigo
- **R** Rice

GRAND BANKS

ATLANTIC OCEAN

PART OF MASSACHUSETTS

NEW HAMPSHIRE

Portsmouth
Salem
Boston
MASS.
Provincetown
New Bedford
CONN. R.I.

NEW YORK

New York
NEW JERSEY
Philadelphia
PENNSYLVANIA
Valley Forge
MD.
Baltimore
DEL.
VIRGINIA
Jamestown
Norfolk
NORTH CAROLINA
Wilmington
SOUTH CAROLINA
Charleston
GEORGIA
Savannah

© RMCN & CO

a

Triangular Trade Routes about 1770

0   500   1000 miles

GREAT BRITAIN
EUROPE

NORTH AMERICA
English Colonies

manufactured goods

sugar, molasses

rum

ATLANTIC OCEAN

AFRICA

grain
livestock
sugar, molasses

WEST INDIES

slaves (Middle Passage)

GOLD COAST

SOUTH AMERICA

b

▲ *Some colonial trade involved the exchange of goods for slaves. Thousands of unwilling immigrants from Africa suffered terribly during the voyage to America.*

Forming a New Nation

Between 1775 and 1800, the United States became an independent nation and established a new government. The Revolutionary War began when American minutemen clashed with British soldiers at Lexington and Concord in 1775. It ended in 1781 when Washington's troops, aided by French forces, defeated Cornwallis and his British troops at Yorktown.

The Treaty of Paris of 1783 recognized the independence of the United States and established its borders. The nation extended from the Atlantic Coast to the Mississippi River. The new states **ceded**, or gave up, their western lands to the federal government. The government created the Northwest Territory and provided for the sale of land to settlers.

The Constitution, ratified in 1788, established the government that remains in effect today. The census in 1790 indicated the national origins of the American population.

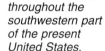
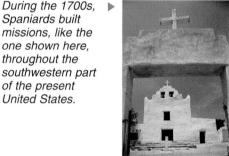

This statue in Boston honors Paul Revere's historic ride on April 18, 1775. Revere rode from Boston to Lexington to warn colonists that the British were coming.

During the 1700s, Spaniards built missions, like the one shown here, throughout the southwestern part of the present United States.

Population by National Origin, 1790

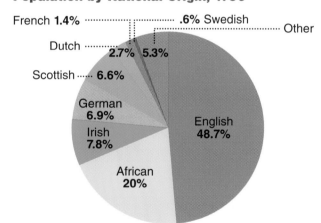

French **1.4%**
.6% Swedish
Other
Dutch
2.7% **5.3%**
Scottish **6.6%**
German **6.9%**
Irish **7.8%**
African **20%**
English **48.7%**

Did You Know **?**

The states carved from the Northwest Territory might be different if Thomas Jefferson had named them. He suggested such names as Dolypotamia, Assinisippia, and Metropotamia.

	1776	1789	1791
People	Juan Bautista de Anza establishes a presidio at San Francisco.	George Washington takes presidential oath of office in New York.	Benjamin Banneker, an African American surveyor, helps plan Washington, D.C.

	1776	1785	1800
Events	Declaration of Independence is signed in Philadelphia.	Land Ordinance provides plan for sale of land in the Northwest Territory.	Washington, D.C. becomes the national capital.

	1776	1782	1787
Literature	"To His Excellency, General Washington," by a slave named Phillis Wheatley, is printed in the Pennsylvania Magazine.	*Letters from an American Farmer*, by Jean de Crèvecoeur, describes social customs in the United States.	*The Federalist*, by Hamilton, Madison, and Jay, urges New York to ratify the Constitution.

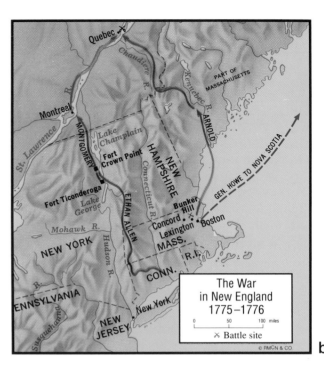

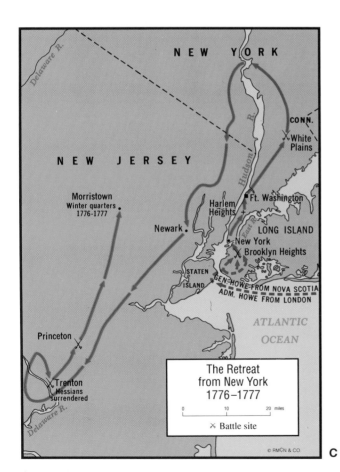

The Battles of
Lexington and Concord
1775

▲ On the way to Concord, the British were met at Lexington by minutemen who had been warned by William Dawes and Paul Revere.

The War
in New England
1775–1776

▲ Americans captured British artillery at Forts Ticonderoga and Crown Point. They used the cannons in Boston, where they forced General William Howe and his troops to leave. An American invasion of Canada, led by General Richard Montgomery and Benedict Arnold, failed.

The Retreat
from New York
1776–1777

▲ The British victory on Long Island forced George Washington and his troops to retreat from New York. After victories at Trenton and Princeton, American troops moved to winter quarters at Morristown.

Clark's Route
1778–1779

▲ Troops led by George Rogers Clark captured British settlements in the Ohio Valley.

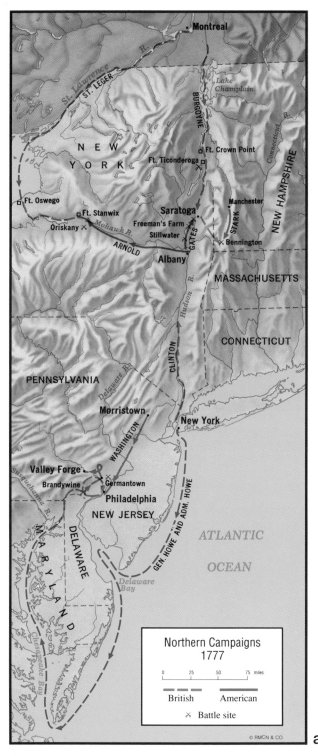

British troops sailed to major ports in the South.

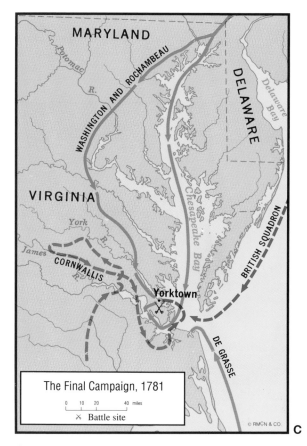

Americans suffered heavy losses at Philadelphia and Germantown, but their victory at Saratoga convinced France to enter the war on the American side.

The war ended at Yorktown when General Charles Cornwallis and his troops surrendered.

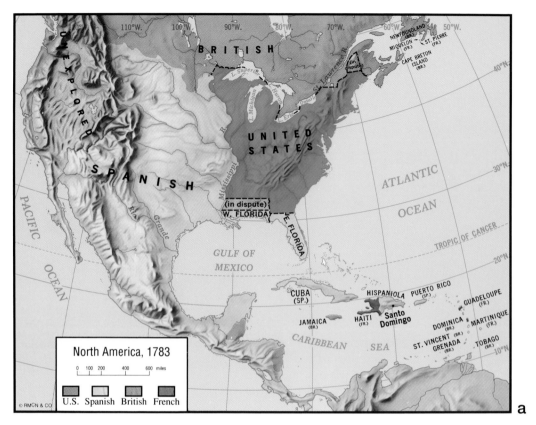

▲ *The Treaty of Paris of 1783 established the boundaries of the United States. The new nation extended from the Atlantic Ocean to the Mississippi River and from 31° north latitude to the Canadian border. The treaty granted Florida to Spain.*

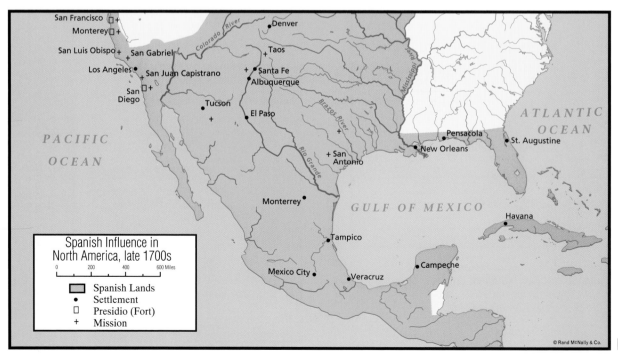

▲ *Spaniards established forts to protect their lands and missions to spread their faith.*

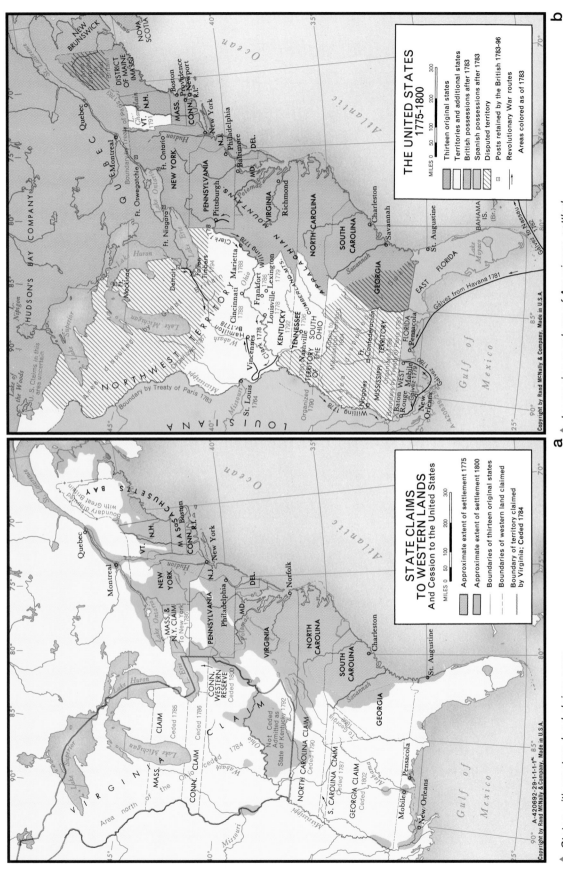

THE UNITED STATES
1775-1800

MILES 0 50 100 200 300

- Thirteen original states
- Territories and additional states
- British possessions after 1783
- Spanish possessions after 1783
- Disputed territory
- Posts retained by the British 1783-96
- Revolutionary War routes
- Areas colored as of 1783

Copyright by Rand McNally & Company, Made in U.S.A.

a ▲ *Increasing numbers of Americans settled west of the Appalachians. Kentucky and Tennessee became states. Britain and Spain disputed areas of land added to the United States in 1783.*

STATE CLAIMS
TO WESTERN LANDS
And Cession to the United States

MILES 0 50 100 200 300

- Approximate extent of settlement 1775
- Approximate extent of settlement 1800
- Boundaries of thirteen original states
- Boundary of western land claimed
- Boundary of territory claimed by Virginia; Ceded 1784

A-420692-29-1-1-1-1▲ Copyright by Rand McNally & Company, Made in U.S.A.

▲ *States with western land claims were asked to put the good of the country above their own interests. Virginia was first to give up its claims. By 1802 all states had ceded their western lands to the United States.*

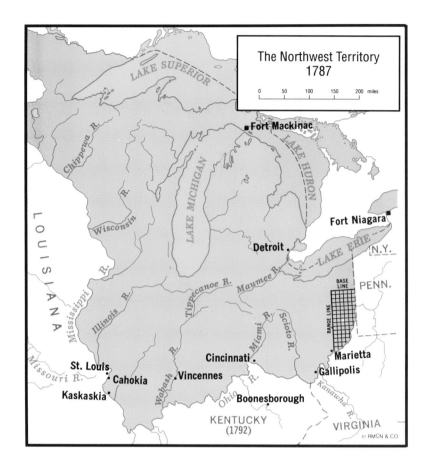

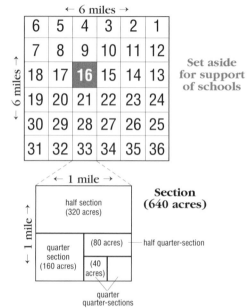

Township

← 6 miles →

6	5	4	3	2	1
7	8	9	10	11	12
18	17	**16**	15	14	13
19	20	21	22	23	24
30	29	28	27	26	25
31	32	33	34	35	36

← 6 miles →

Set aside for support of schools

← 1 mile →

← 1 mile →

half section (320 acres)

quarter section (160 acres)

(80 acres) — half quarter-section

(40 acres)

quarter quarter-sections

Section (640 acres)

The Northwest Territory was land north of the Ohio River that later became the states of Ohio, Indiana, Illinois, Michigan, and Wisconsin. The Land Ordinance of 1785 provided a plan for the sale of this land.

Public lands were divided into townships that were six miles square. The white square on the map represents one township. Each township was divided into 36 sections, as shown on the diagram. Each section consisted of 640 acres, and it sold for $1 per acre.

In the 1780s, few settlers could afford to buy a section of land. Companies such as the Ohio Company and Scioto Company bought land from the government and divided it into smaller lots. Then they sold it to settlers at a profit.

Section 16 in each township was set aside by the government for the support of education. Settlers could rent or sell this land to raise money for public schools.

Section 4   *(1790-1870)*

The Nation Expands & Changes

Between 1790 and 1870, the United States expanded its boundaries to the Pacific Coast. Through the Louisiana Purchase in 1803, it acquired the vast land between the Mississippi River and the Rocky Mountains. Through war with Mexico, 1846-1848, it gained land in the Southwest. Through a treaty with Britain in 1846, it gained land in the Pacific Northwest. Within 70 years after the United States became an independent nation, it had tripled in size.

Explorers, trappers, and traders blazed trails to the West. Pioneers rapidly settled new territories, pushing the **frontier**, or edge of settled land, west of the Mississippi River. Settlers followed the Oregon Trail to the Pacific Northwest. Mormons traveled to Utah in search of religious freedom. Gold seekers poured into California. Millions of immigrants from Europe came to the United States seeking a better life.

◀ *The Gateway Arch stands along the Mississippi River in St. Louis. It honors the Louisiana Purchase and the pioneers who settled the West.*

This monument ▶ marks the Oregon Trail, which thousands of pioneers traveled from Independence, Missouri, to the Oregon country.

Did You Know
?

Francis Scott Key wrote "The Star-Spangled Banner" during the War of 1812 as he watched the bombardment of Fort McHenry from a ship in Baltimore Harbor. The words were set to music and later became our national anthem.

Area of Selected Lands Added to the United States, 1803-1867

1803	Louisiana Purchase
1845	Texas Annexation
1846	Oregon Treaty
1848	Mexican Cession
1867	Alaska Purchase

0   200   400   600
Millions of acres

	1803	**1847**	**1848**
People	President Thomas Jefferson purchases Louisiana Territory from France.	Brigham Young leads Mormon migration from Illinois to the Great Salt Lake.	Elizabeth Cady Stanton and Lucretia Mott hold women's rights convention in New York.
	1819	**1825**	**1849**
Events	United States acquires Florida from Spain.	Erie Canal links the Great Lakes and Atlantic Ocean.	Gold rush brings thousands of people to California.
	1820	**1827**	**1854**
Literature	"Rip Van Winkle," by Washington Irving, is set in the Catskill Mountains.	*The Prairie*, by James Fenimore Cooper, describes frontier life on the western plains.	*Walden*, by Henry David Thoreau, describes the beauty of nature in Massachusetts.

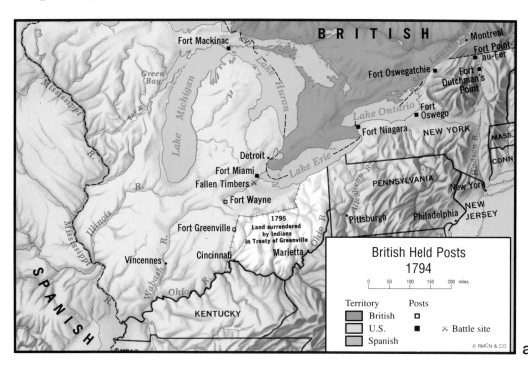

◄ *According to the Treaty of Greenville, Indians gave up claims to land in the Northwest Territory. The British violated the Treaty of Paris of 1783 by keeping posts in U.S. territory.*

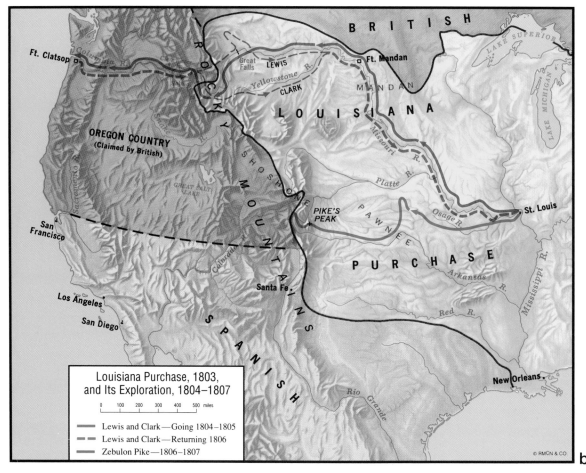

▲ *Explorations of the Louisiana Purchase by Lewis and Clark and Pike provided valuable information about lands west of the Mississippi River.*

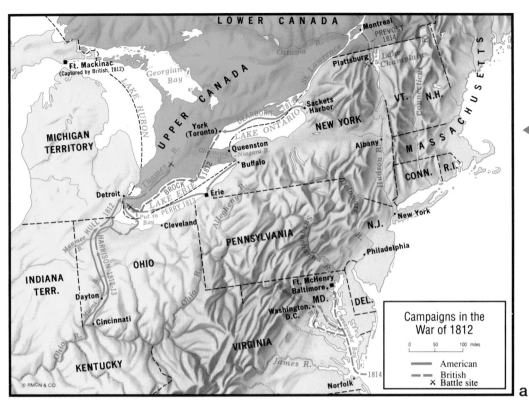

Campaigns in the War of 1812 were widely scattered. They included a decisive U.S. victory on Lake Erie as well as the British capture and burning of Washington, D.C.

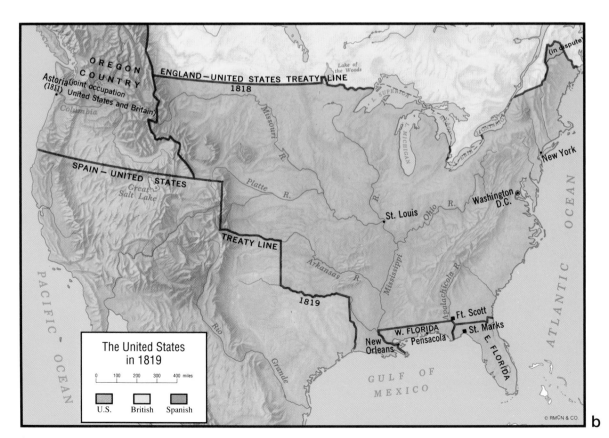

The Treaty of Ghent set a boundary between U.S. and British lands and allowed both nations to settle the Oregon Country. The Adams-Onís Treaty set a boundary between U.S. and Spanish lands and gave Florida to the United States.

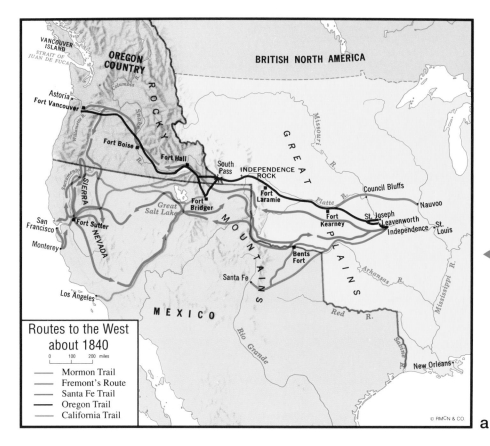

The constant traffic of settlers to the Oregon Country marked a trail across the Great Plains and Rocky Mountains. Traders and trappers blazed other trails that settlers later followed to the Far West.

Routes to the West about 1840

0   100   200 miles

— Mormon Trail
— Fremont's Route
— Santa Fe Trail
— Oregon Trail
— California Trail

© RMCN & CO.

a

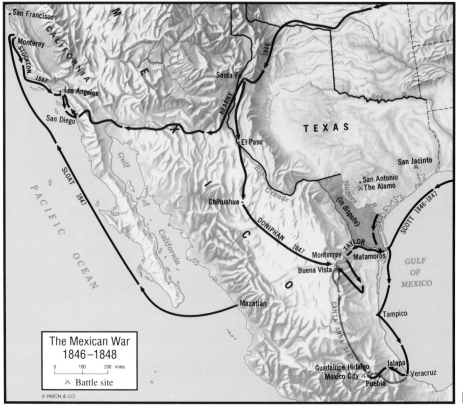

The Mexican War 1846–1848

0   100   200 miles

✕ Battle site

© RMCN & CO.

The Mexican War began with a dispute over the southern boundary of Texas—the area shown in pink on the map. It ended when General Winfield Scott defeated Santa Anna and captured Mexico City. As a result of this war, the United States gained a large territory in the southwest.

b

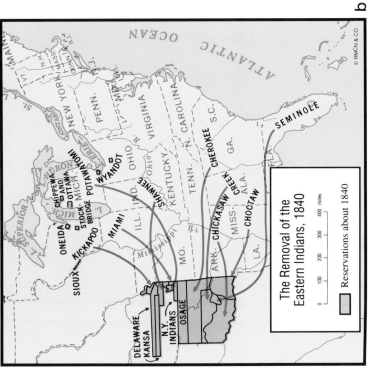

The Removal of the
Eastern Indians, 1840

	Reservations about 1840

0 100 200 300 400 miles

© RMCN & CO

▲ The U.S. government forced Native
Americans to leave their lands in the
East and move to reservations in the
West. The journey of 15,000 Cherokees
from Georgia to Oklahoma became
known as the Trail of Tears. About 4,000
Indians died along the way.

b

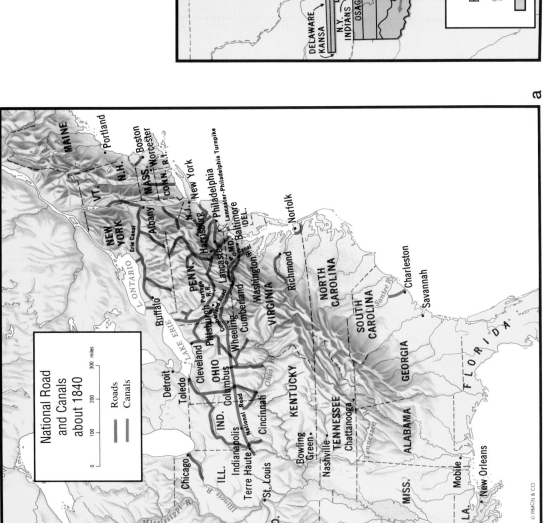

National Road
and Canals
about 1840

Roads
Canals

0 100 200 300 miles

© RMCN & CO

▲ The Cumberland Road, also called the
National Road, extended from Maryland
to Illinois. The Erie Canal provided a
link between the Great Lakes and the
Atlantic Ocean.

a

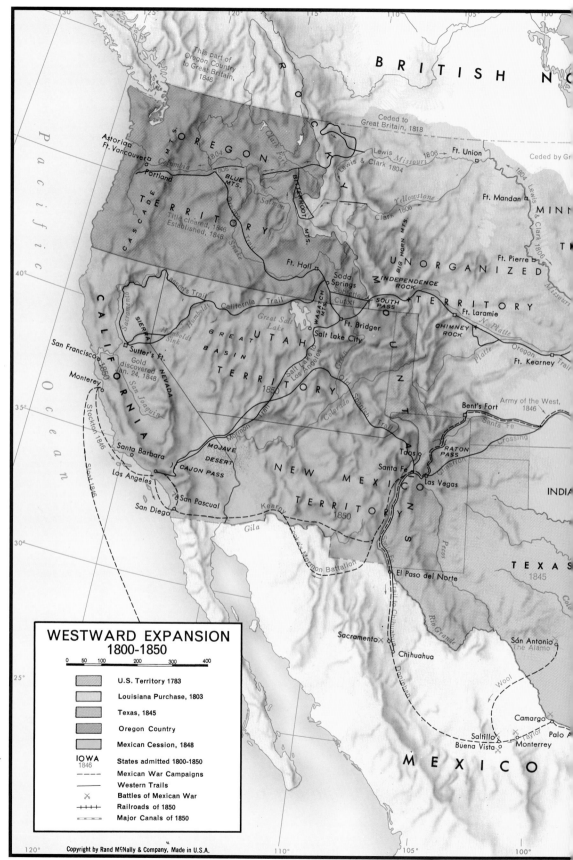

Between 1800 ► and 1850, the United States added fifteen new states and extended its borders to the Pacific Coast.

WESTWARD EXPANSION
1800-1850

0 50 100   200   300   400

U.S. Territory 1783
Louisiana Purchase, 1803
Texas, 1845
Oregon Country
Mexican Cession, 1848

IOWA   States admitted 1800-1850
1846
------   Mexican War Campaigns
———   Western Trails
×   Battles of Mexican War
++++   Railroads of 1850
- - -   Major Canals of 1850

Copyright by Rand McNally & Company, Made in U.S.A.

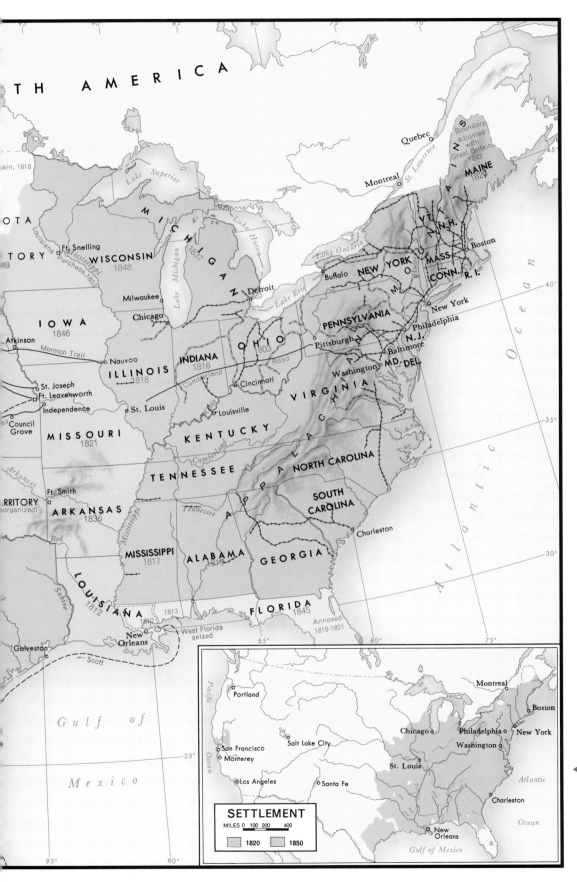

NORTH AMERICA

Quebec

Montreal

St. Lawrence

Boundary adjusted with Great Britain 1842

MAINE 1824

Lake Superior

Ft. Snelling

MINNESOTA TERRITORY 1849

Louisiana Purchase 1803

MICHIGAN 1837

WISCONSIN 1848

Lake Michigan

Lake Huron

Lake Ontario

Buffalo

NEW YORK

VT.

N.H.

MASS.

CONN.

R.I.

Boston

Milwaukee

Chicago

Detroit

Lake Erie

Hudson

New York

IOWA 1846

Atkinson

Mormon Trail

Nauvoo

ILLINOIS 1818

INDIANA 1816

OHIO 1803

Cumberland Road

PENNSYLVANIA

Pittsburgh

Philadelphia

N.J.

Baltimore

MD. DEL.

St. Joseph

Ft. Leavenworth

Independence

St. Louis

Cincinnati

Louisville

Ohio

Washington

VIRGINIA

Council Grove

MISSOURI 1821

KENTUCKY

Cumberland

APPALACHIANS

TENNESSEE

Tennessee

NORTH CAROLINA

Ft. Smith

INDIAN TERRITORY (not organized)

ARKANSAS 1836

Mississippi

Red

SOUTH CAROLINA

Charleston

Arkansas

MISSISSIPPI 1817

ALABAMA 1819

GEORGIA

LOUISIANA 1812

Sabine

1813

1810

New Orleans

West Florida seized

FLORIDA 1845

Annexed 1819-1821

Galveston

Scott

Gulf of Mexico

Atlantic Ocean

SETTLEMENT

MILES 0 100 200 400

1820   1850

Portland

San Francisco

Monterey

Los Angeles

Pacific Ocean

Salt Lake City

Santa Fe

Chicago

St. Louis

New Orleans

Montreal

Boston

Philadelphia

New York

Washington

Charleston

Atlantic Ocean

Gulf of Mexico

◄ By 1850 settlement had spread west of the Mississippi River. Thousands of settlers also moved to the Far West.

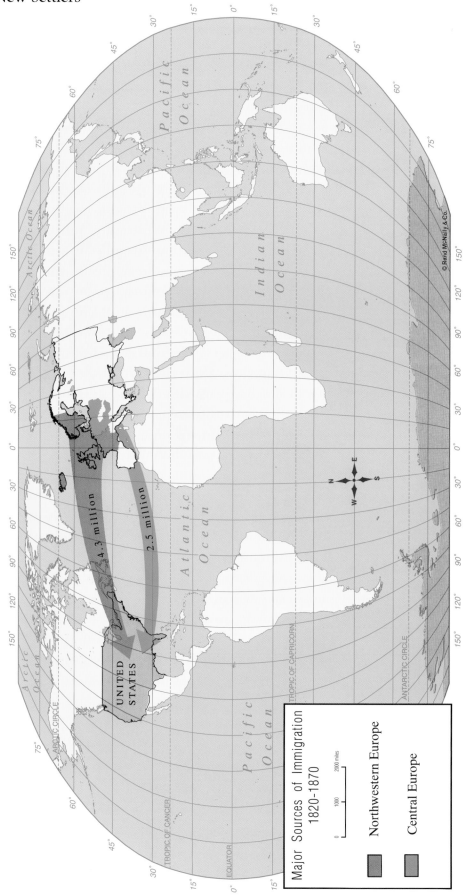

▲ *Between 1820 and 1870, about 7.5 million immigrants came to the United States. Most came from northern and western Europe. Crop failure and poverty led Irish, German, and Scandinavian immigrants to seek a better life in America.*

Major Sources of Immigration
1820-1870

Northwestern Europe

Central Europe

4.3 million

2.5 million

UNITED STATES

© Rand McNally & Co.

Section 5 (1850-1865)

A Nation Divided

Between 1850 and 1860, differences between the North and the South widened. The agricultural economy of the South was based on slave labor. Many Northerners viewed slavery as wrong. **Abolitionists**, or people who demanded an end to slavery, operated the Underground Railroad to help slaves escape. The Compromise of 1850 and the Kansas-Nebraska Act attempted to settle the issue of slavery in the West.

When Abraham Lincoln was elected president in 1860, Southerners feared he would end slavery. Eleven southern states **seceded**, or withdrew, from the Union and formed the Confederacy. An attack on Fort Sumter in April 1861 marked the beginning of the Civil War. The war ended when Confederate general Robert E. Lee surrendered at Appomattox in April 1865.

The bitter war between the North and the South left lasting problems. Much of the South was destroyed. More Americans lost their lives in the Civil War than in any other war in which the United States has fought.

◄ The Battle of Gettysburg took place at this site in Pennsylvania in July 1863.

◄ This memorial to Confederate leaders is carved on Stone Mountain near Atlanta, Georgia.

American Deaths in Major Wars

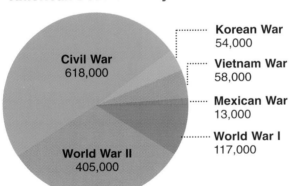

Civil War 618,000

World War II 405,000

Korean War 54,000

Vietnam War 58,000

Mexican War 13,000

World War I 117,000

Did You Know ?

When Virginia seceded from the Union in 1861, 50 of its western counties separated from the state. These counties were admitted to the Union in 1863 as the state of West Virginia.

	1850	1863	1865
People	Harriet Tubman leads slaves from Maryland to freedom in the North.	Abraham Lincoln delivers Gettysburg Address on battlefield in Pennsylvania.	Robert E. Lee surrenders at Appomattox Court House, Virginia.

	1860	1861	1865
Events	South Carolina becomes first southern state to secede.	Civil War begins at Fort Sumter, South Carolina.	Thirteenth Amendment ends slavery in the United States.

	1850	1852	1865
Literature	*The Scarlet Letter*, by Nathaniel Hawthorne, is set in Puritan New England.	*Uncle Tom's Cabin*, by Harriet Beecher Stowe, highlights the cruelty of slavery in the South.	"Drum Taps," by Walt Whitman, describes scenes from Civil War battlefields.

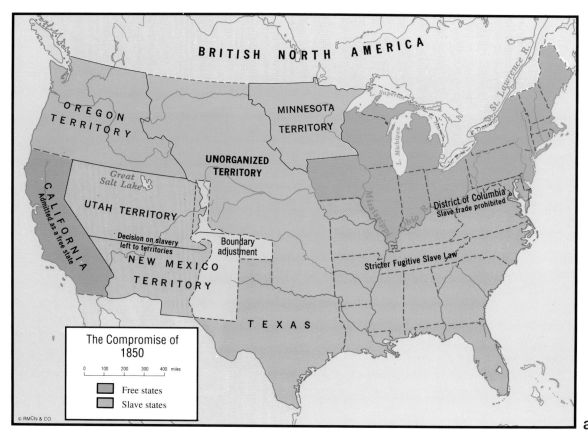

The Compromise of 1850

0 100 200 300 400 miles

Free states
Slave states

▲ *The Compromise of 1850 admitted California as a free state and ended slave trade in the District of Columbia. Utah and New Mexico Territories could decide the issue of slavery.*

Kansas–Nebraska Act, 1854

0 100 200 300 miles

▲ *The Kansas-Nebraska Act allowed settlers in those territories to decide whether to allow slavery.*

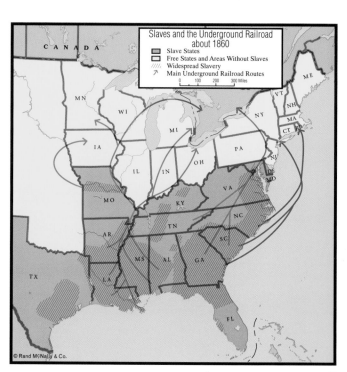

Slaves and the Underground Railroad
about 1860

Slave States
Free States and Areas Without Slaves
Widespread Slavery
Main Underground Railroad Routes

0 100 200 300 Miles

▲ *The Underground Railroad was a system of escape routes slaves followed to freedom.*

41

A Quarreling People
1820-1860

▲ Economic differences created different ways of life in the North and the South. Plantation crops, such as tobacco, cotton, and sugar cane, supported an agricultural economy based on slavery in the South. Advances in mass production and transportation supported an economy based on industry and trade in the North. Northern abolitionists viewed slavery as wrong and began a movement to end it.

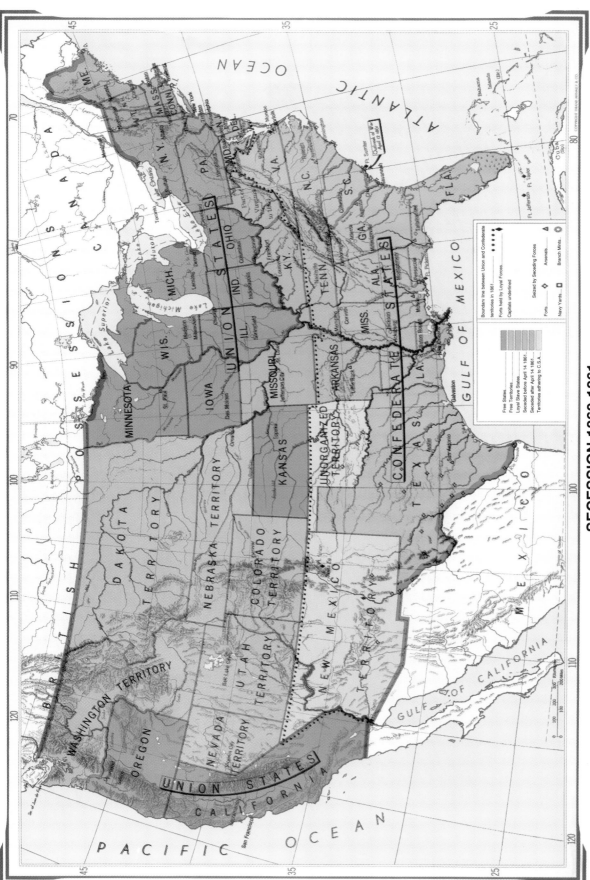

SECESSION 1860-1861

▲ The Confederate States of America consisted of eleven slave states that seceded from the Union in 1860 and 1861. The 23 remaining states and territories, including four slave states, fought for the Union during the Civil War.

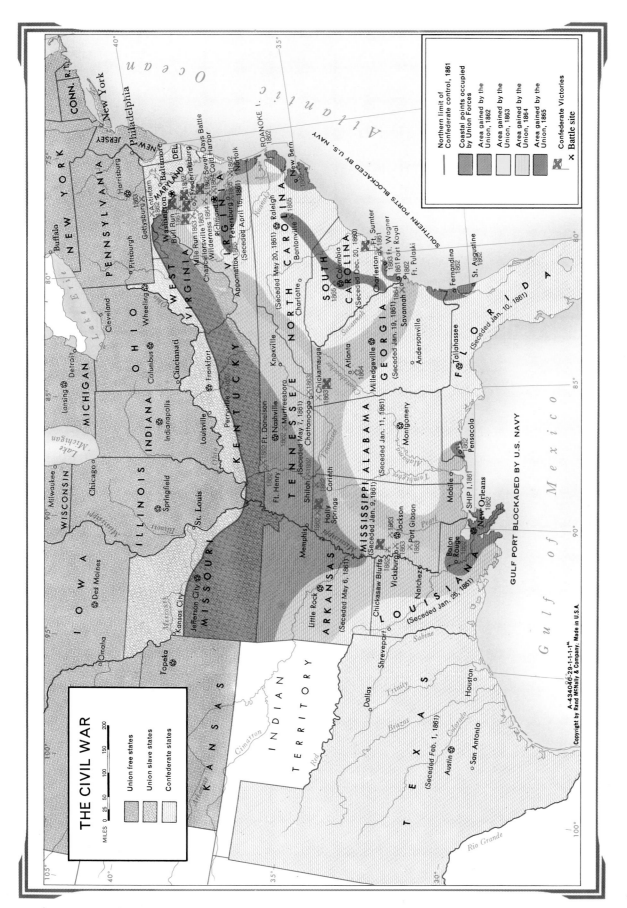

THE CIVIL WAR

MILES 0 25 50 100 150 200

- Union free states
- Union slave states
- Confederate states

Legend

- Northern limit of Confederate control, 1861
- Coastal points occupied by Union Forces
- Area gained by the Union, 1862
- Area gained by the Union, 1863
- Area gained by the Union, 1864
- Area gained by the Union, 1865
- Confederate Victories
- × Battle site

Most of the fighting in the East took place in Virginia. Much of the fighting in the West took place in Tennessee and along the Mississippi River. The map legend indicates how Union strategy succeeded by dividing the Confederacy and blockading its ports.

A-434046-29-1-1-1-1^A
Copyright by Rand McNally & Company. Made in U.S.A.

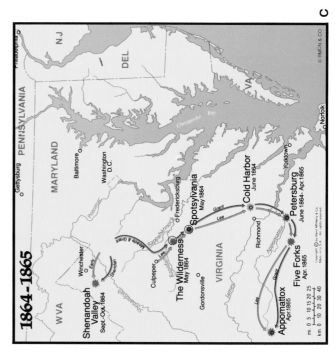

1864-1865

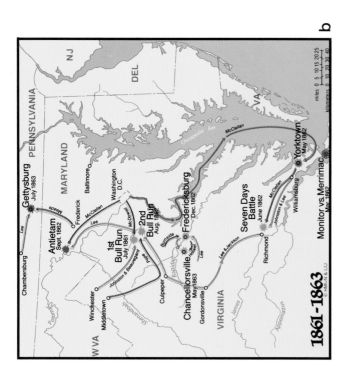

1861-1863

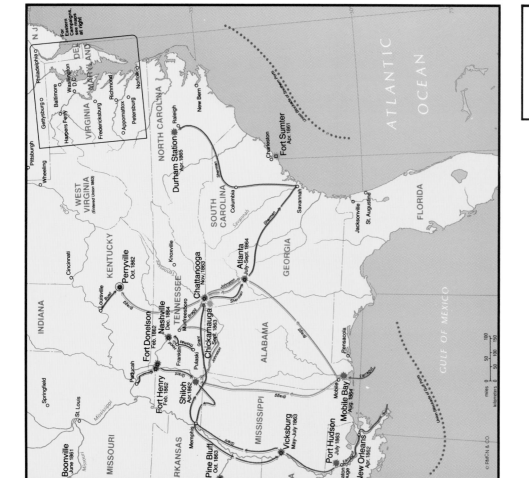

The Civil War
1861–1865

- Union victory
- Confederate victory
- Battle indecisive
- Union forces
- Confederate forces

Union strategy involved blockading southern ports, splitting the Confederacy by gaining control of the Mississippi River Valley, and capturing Richmond. Confederate strategy involved defending the South from attack, breaking the Union blockade, and splitting the Union by gaining control of Washington, D.C., Maryland, and central Pennsylvania.

Section 6   *(1860-1920)*

Emerging as a Modern Nation

The years between 1860 and 1920 included the end of one era in American history and the beginning of another. The Great Plains opened to settlers as the U.S. Army defeated the Plains Indians and forced them onto reservations. Texas cattle ranchers drove their herds to railroads, which provided transportation to eastern markets. **Homesteaders**, or settlers who received free land from the government in exchange for farming it, moved to western territories. By 1890, the long process of settling the United States from coast to coast was complete. The American frontier had come to an end.

In the late 1800s, the United States began to emerge as a modern nation. Millions of immigrants came from Europe to farm the land or work in factories. The United States became an industrial nation and acquired territories overseas. It purchased Alaska and established naval bases on islands in the Pacific. It fought a war with Spain by which it acquired additional territories. The United States entered World War I in 1917 and assumed its role as a world power.

◀ *This statue of Buffalo Bill Cody in Wyoming represents the Old West.*

The Statue of Liberty ▶ in New York Harbor has welcomed immigrants since 1886. It was a gift to the United States from France.

Immigration to the United States, 1860-1919

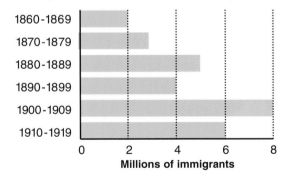

	Millions of immigrants
1860-1869	
1870-1879	
1880-1889	
1890-1899	
1900-1909	
1910-1919	

Did You Know

?

In 1850 about 20 million bison, or buffaloes, roamed the Great Plains. The westward movement almost wiped out these animals. By 1890, only about 500 bison could be found in the West.

	1877	**1889**	**1898**
People	Chief Joseph leads Nez Percés on a retreat through Idaho and Montana.	Jane Addams opens Hull House to help immigrants in Chicago.	Theodore Roosevelt leads Rough Riders in Cuba during Spanish-American War.

	1867	**1892**	**1898**
Events	United States purchases Alaska from Russia.	Ellis Island, in New York Harbor, becomes an immigration station.	Hawaii becomes a U. S. territory.

	1876	**1881**	**1912**
Literature	*The Adventures of Tom Sawyer,* by Mark Twain, is set in Hannibal, Missouri.	*A Century of Dishonor,* by Helen Hunt Jackson, describes mistreatment of Native Americans in the U.S.	*Riders of the Purple Sage*, by Zane Grey, describes life in the West.

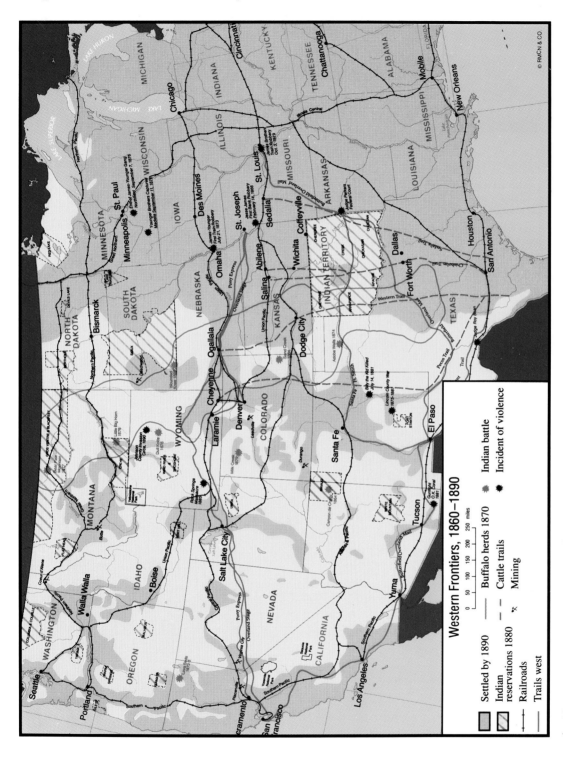

Western Frontiers, 1860–1890

☐ Settled by 1890	— Buffalo herds 1870	✳ Indian battle
▨ Indian reservations 1880	– – Cattle trails	✳ Incident of violence
	✕ Mining	
+—+ Railroads		
— Trails west		

0 50 100 150 200 250 miles

▲ *After 1860, the population west of the Mississippi River grew rapidly. Native Americans lost the battle to keep their lands, and the government moved them to reservations. Ranchers and farmers spread settlements throughout the Great Plains and the Far West. Although large areas of the West remained thinly populated, in 1890 the Census Bureau declared the frontier had come to an end.*

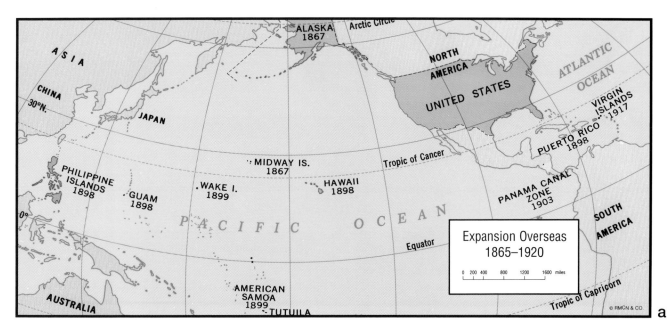

Expansion Overseas
1865–1920

0   200 400   800   1200   1600 miles

a

▲ The United States acquired islands in the Pacific Ocean that served as fueling
stations for ships traveling to and from China and Japan. The Hawaiian Islands
also provided raw materials for import or trade.

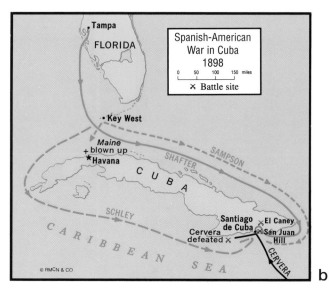

Spanish-American
War in Cuba
1898

0   50   100   150 miles

✕ Battle site

b

▲ The sinking of the American battleship
Maine in Havana harbor brought the
United States into war with Spain. The
war was fought in both Cuba and the
Philippines. As a result of the Spanish-
American War, Spain granted freedom
to Cuba and ceded Guam, Puerto Rico,
and the Philippines to the United States.

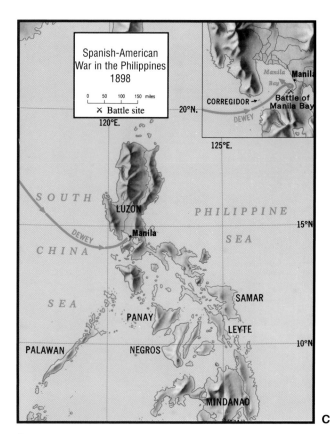

Spanish-American
War in the Philippines
1898

0   50   100   150 miles

✕ Battle site

c

▲ In the Battle of Manila Bay, American
ships commanded by Commodore George
Dewey destroyed the Spanish fleet in the
Philippines.

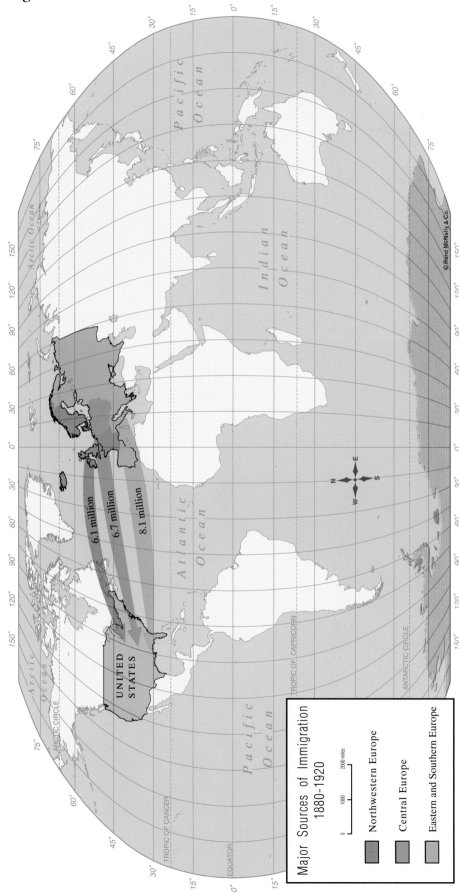

Major Sources of Immigration 1880–1920

- Northwestern Europe
- Central Europe
- Eastern and Southern Europe

6.1 million
6.7 million
8.1 million

UNITED STATES

▲ Between 1880 and 1920, more than 20 million immigrants came to the United States. Unlike earlier newcomers, who came mostly from northern and western Europe, these so-called "new immigrants" came mostly from central, eastern, and southern Europe.

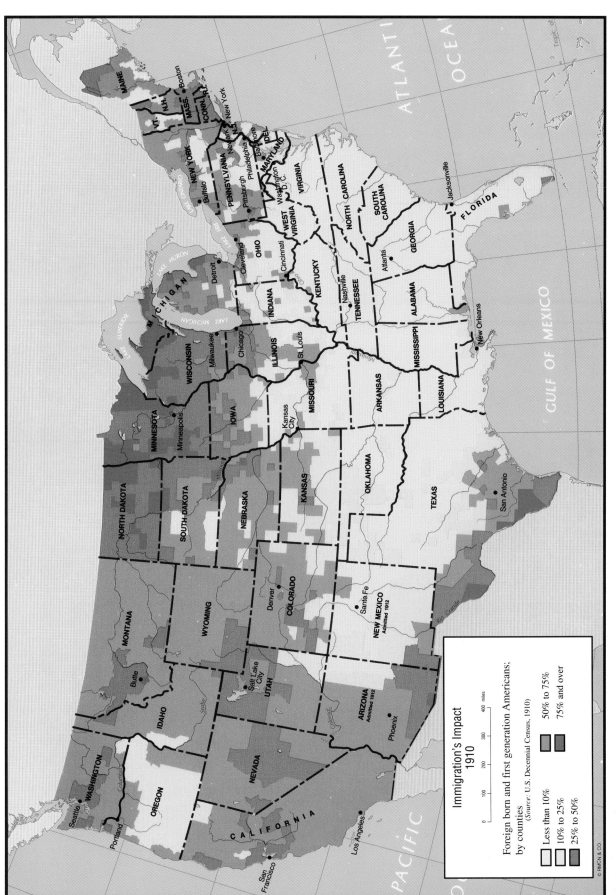

▲ *Many immigrants settled in large cities in the East. Mining attracted newcomers to Montana, Colorado, and Nevada. Railroad companies encouraged European workers to settle in the West. Poor economic conditions in Mexico led thousands of immigrants to settle in the United States.*

Immigration's Impact 1910

Foreign born and first generation Americans; by counties
(*Source:* U.S. Decennial Census, 1910)

Less than 10%
10% to 25%
25% to 50%
50% to 75%
75% and over

0 100 200 300 400 miles

© RMCN & CO.

ATLANTIC OCEAN

MAINE
N.H.
VT.
MASS.
Boston
CONN. R.I.
NEW YORK
Newark New York
PENNSYLVANIA
Buffalo
Pittsburgh
Philadelphia
Baltimore
DEL.
MARYLAND
Washington D.C.
WEST VIRGINIA
VIRGINIA
OHIO
Cleveland
Cincinnati
NORTH CAROLINA
SOUTH CAROLINA
GEORGIA
Atlanta
FLORIDA
Jacksonville
MICHIGAN
Detroit
KENTUCKY
Nashville
TENNESSEE
ALABAMA
MISSISSIPPI
INDIANA
ILLINOIS
Chicago
St. Louis
Milwaukee
WISCONSIN
MINNESOTA
Minneapolis
IOWA
MISSOURI
Kansas City
ARKANSAS
LOUISIANA
New Orleans
GULF OF MEXICO
NORTH DAKOTA
SOUTH DAKOTA
NEBRASKA
KANSAS
OKLAHOMA
TEXAS
San Antonio
MONTANA
Butte
WYOMING
COLORADO
Denver
NEW MEXICO
Admitted 1912
Santa Fe
Rio Grande
IDAHO
UTAH
Salt Lake City
ARIZONA
Admitted 1912
Phoenix
NEVADA
CALIFORNIA
Los Angeles
San Francisco
WASHINGTON
Seattle
OREGON
Portland
Columbia
PACIFIC

▲ *In 1914, long-standing problems in Europe erupted in war between the Allied Powers and the Central Powers. The conflict, which became known as World War I, lasted four years. It involved more countries and caused more destruction than had any previous war.*

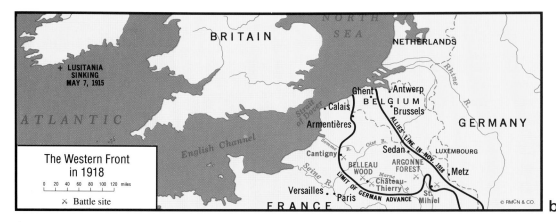

▲ *The loss of American lives aboard the* Lusitania *helped draw the United States into the war in Europe. American troops helped the Allies defeat the Germans on the Western Front, which stretched through Belgium and France.*

Section 7 (1920-1990)

Challenges & Changes in the 20th Century

During the decades between 1920 and 1990, the United States faced many challenges and experienced many changes. The economic prosperity of the 1920s ended with the stock market crash in 1929. Poverty and unemployment were widespread during the Great Depression of the 1930s. During World War II (1941-1945), United States troops fought in Europe and in the Pacific. After this war, the United States and the Soviet Union emerged as the world's leading powers.

The struggle between the Communist world, led by the Soviet Union, and the free world, led by the United States, was called the **Cold War**. Between 1950 and 1990, the United States intervened in Korea, in Southeast Asia, and in Central America and the Caribbean to stop the spread of communism.

Changes took place within the United States as Americans moved from one area of the country to another, and suburbs grew around major cities. The **gross domestic product** (GDP), or value of all goods and services produced within the country, rose sharply after 1940. Economic growth continued into the 1990s.

◄ The United States Marine Corps Memorial in Arlington, Virginia, honors the flag raising on Iwo Jima during World War II.

◄ In 1940 Houston, Texas, ranked 21st in population among U.S. cities. By 1990, it was among the nation's largest metropolitan areas.

Gross Domestic Product, 1920-1990

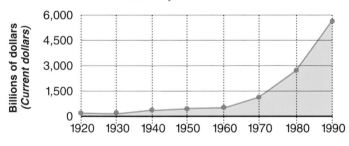

Billions of dollars (Current dollars)

6,000 / 4,500 / 3,000 / 1,500 / 0

1920 1930 1940 1950 1960 1970 1980 1990

Did You Know?

Between 1941 and 1945, one in every five Americans moved from one part of the United States to another.

	1927	**1963**	**1981**
People	Charles Lindbergh makes first nonstop flight from New York to Paris.	Dr. Martin Luther King, Jr., leads civil rights march on Washington, D.C.	Arizona judge Sandra Day O'Connor becomes first woman to serve on the Supreme Court.
	1959	**1961**	**1973**
Events	Alaska and Hawaii become states.	First American astronaut is launched into space from Cape Canaveral, Florida.	Native Americans seize Wounded Knee, South Dakota, to demand return of Indian lands.
	1939	**1961**	**1971**
Literature	*The Grapes of Wrath*, by John Steinbeck, tells of an Oklahoma family during the Great Depression.	*To Kill a Mockingbird*, by Harper Lee, explores racial prejudice in Alabama.	*Barrio Boy*, by Ernesto Galarza, describes Hispanic life in Sacramento, California.

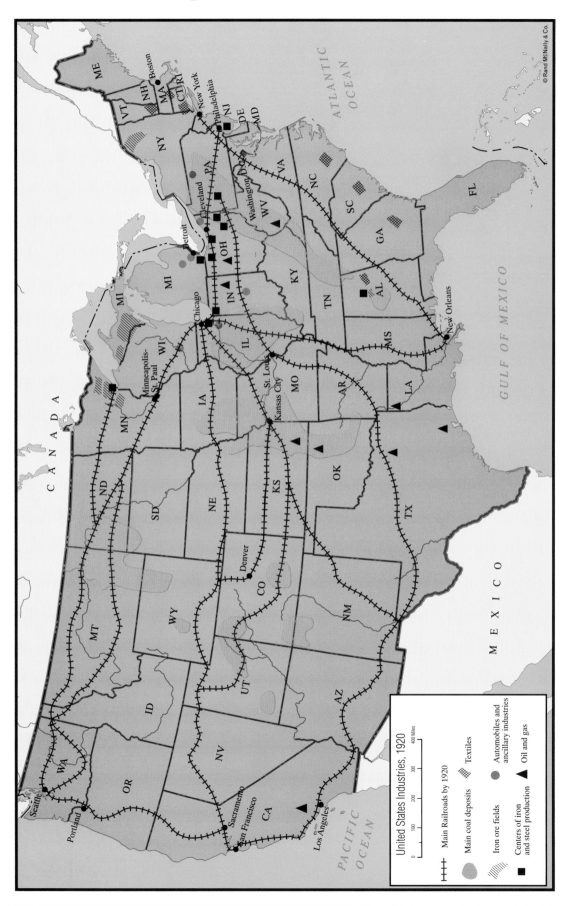

▲ By 1920 the United States was a leading industrial nation. Advances in technology enabled workers to produce more goods faster. The demand for petroleum and steel increased to meet the growing needs of new industries such as the automobile industry. Spectacular economic growth provided a high standard of living for many Americans.

United States Industries, 1920

0   100   200   300   400 Miles

Main Railroads by 1920

Main coal deposits   Textiles

Iron ore fields   Automobiles and
                                       ancillary industries

Centers of iron   Oil and gas
and steel production

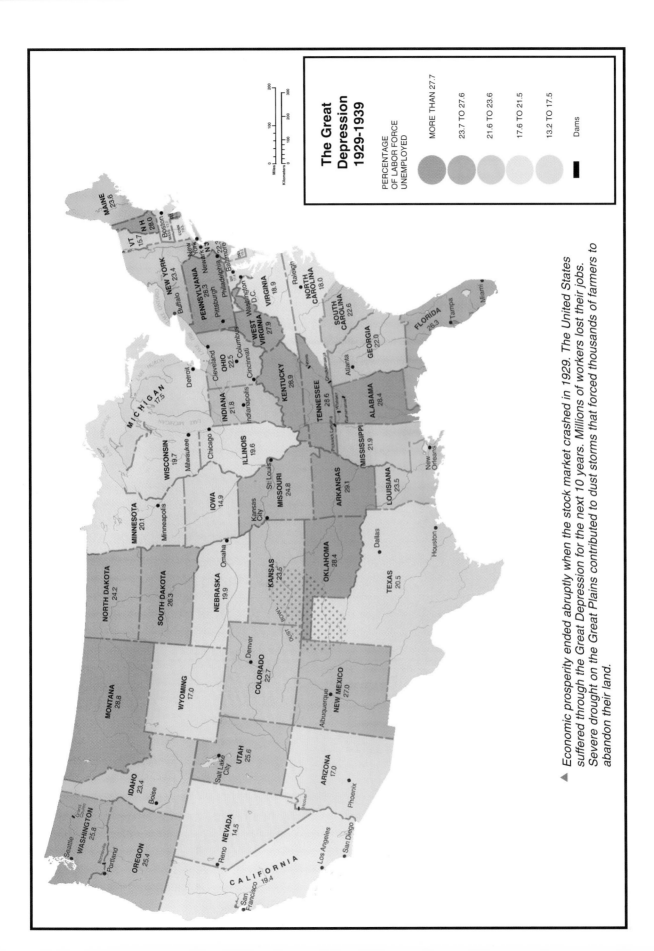

The Great Depression 1929-1939

PERCENTAGE
OF LABOR FORCE
UNEMPLOYED

MORE THAN 27.7

23.7 TO 27.6

21.6 TO 23.6

17.6 TO 21.5

13.2 TO 17.5

Dams

▲ Economic prosperity ended abruptly when the stock market crashed in 1929. The United States suffered through the Great Depression for the next 10 years. Millions of workers lost their jobs. Severe drought on the Great Plains contributed to dust storms that forced thousands of farmers to abandon their land.

MAINE 23.6

N H 28.0

VT 15.7

NEW YORK 23.4

PENNSYLVANIA 28.3

WEST VIRGINIA 27.9

VIRGINIA 18.9

NORTH CAROLINA 18.0

SOUTH CAROLINA 22.6

GEORGIA 22.0

FLORIDA 26.3

KENTUCKY 28.9

TENNESSEE 28.6

ALABAMA 28.4

MISSISSIPPI 21.9

LOUISIANA 23.5

ARKANSAS 29.1

OHIO 22.5

INDIANA 21.8

ILLINOIS 19.6

MICHIGAN 17.5

WISCONSIN 19.7

IOWA 14.9

MISSOURI 24.8

OKLAHOMA 28.4

TEXAS 20.5

MINNESOTA 20.1

NORTH DAKOTA 24.2

SOUTH DAKOTA 26.3

NEBRASKA 19.9

KANSAS 23.5

COLORADO 22.7

NEW MEXICO 27.0

MONTANA 28.8

WYOMING 17.0

UTAH 25.6

ARIZONA 17.0

IDAHO 23.4

NEVADA 14.5

WASHINGTON 25.8

OREGON 25.4

CALIFORNIA 19.4

Seattle
Portland
San Francisco
Los Angeles
San Diego
Reno
Salt Lake City
Boise
Phoenix
Albuquerque
Denver
Omaha
Kansas City
Minneapolis
Milwaukee
Chicago
St. Louis
Dallas
Houston
New Orleans
Detroit
Cleveland
Cincinnati
Columbus
Indianapolis
Atlanta
Raleigh
Washington D.C.
Baltimore
Philadelphia
Pittsburgh
Buffalo
Newark
New York
Boston
Tampa
Miami

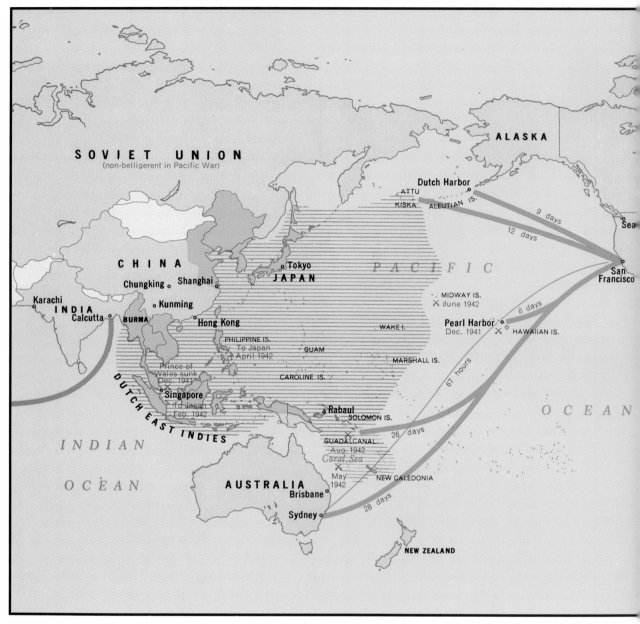

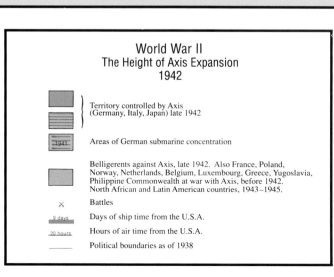

World War II
The Height of Axis Expansion
1942

Territory controlled by Axis
(Germany, Italy, Japan) late 1942

Areas of German submarine concentration

Belligerents against Axis, late 1942. Also France, Poland,
Norway, Netherlands, Belgium, Luxembourg, Greece, Yugoslavia,
Philippine Commonwealth at war with Axis, before 1942.
North African and Latin American countries, 1943–1945.

✕   Battles

Days of ship time from the U.S.A.

Hours of air time from the U.S.A.

Political boundaries as of 1938

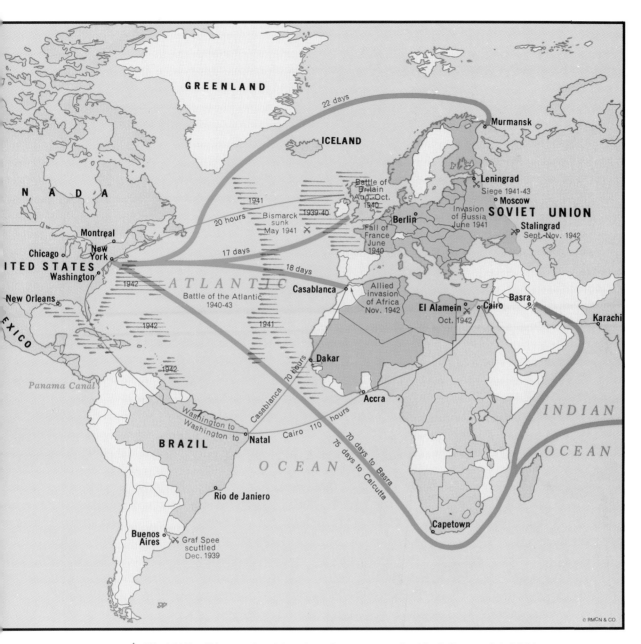

▲ World War II began in 1939 when Germany, under Nazi dictator Adolf Hitler, invaded Poland. The Axis powers (Germany, Italy, Japan, and their partners) fought against the Allied powers (shown in gold on the map). Few nations remained neutral. By 1942 the Axis controlled most of Europe, northern Africa, and parts of Asia and the Pacific. German submarines attacked Allied cargo ships in the Atlantic.

The Japanese attack on Pearl Harbor, Hawaii, in December 1941 brought the United States into the war. American troops and supplies were sent to Europe and to the Pacific. The map indicates transportation time by air and by water from the United States to selected sites. During 1942, Allied forces halted Axis expansion in northern Africa, the Soviet Union, and the Pacific.

SOVIET UNION

ALASKA

Kiska & Attu
June 1942

MONGOLIA   MANCHURIA

JAPAN

KOREA

Peking

Tokyo

CHINA

Hiroshima
Aug. 1945

Midway Island
June 1942

Shanghai

Chungking

Okinawa
Mar.-Apr. 1945

Iwo Jima
Feb. 1945

Wake Island
Dec. 1941

IDIA

Hong Kong

Philippine Sea
June 1944

Saipan, Tinian, & Guam
June-July 1944

BURMA

FRENCH
INDOCHINA

PHILIPPINES

Eniwetok
Feb. 1944

THAILAND

Bataan
Jan.-Feb. 1942

Leyte Gulf
Oct. 1944

Truk Islands
Feb. 1944

Kwajalein
Jan. 1944

MALAYA

BRUNEI   N BORNEO
SARAWAK

Singapore

BORNEO

Hollandia
Apr. 1944

Bougainville
Nov. 1943

Tarawa
Nov. 1943

SUMATRA

NEW GUINEA

Empress Augusta Bay
Nov. 1943

Guadalcanal
Aug. 1942-Feb. 1943

PACIFIC

OCEAN

Equator

INDIAN

OCEAN

Coral Sea
May 1942

AUSTRALIA

miles 0   250   500   750   1000
kilometers 0   500   1000   1500

World War II
1941–1945
Pacific Theater

Allied powers

Axis powers

Battles

Axis controlled
areas

Allied advances

▲ In 1943 and 1944, the Allies captured
Japanese-held islands in the Pacific. In
August 1945, the United States dropped
an atomic bomb on Hiroshima, Japan.
World War II ended when the Japanese
surrendered in September 1945.

▲ After defeating the Axis in northern
Africa, the Allies focused on Europe.
Italy surrendered in 1943. In 1944 Allies
landed in northern France and advanced
on Germany from the west, while Soviet
troops advanced from the east. Germany
surrendered in May 1945.

World War II
1941–1945
European Theater

Allied powers   Neutral nations
Axis powers   Battles
Axis controlled areas   Allied advances

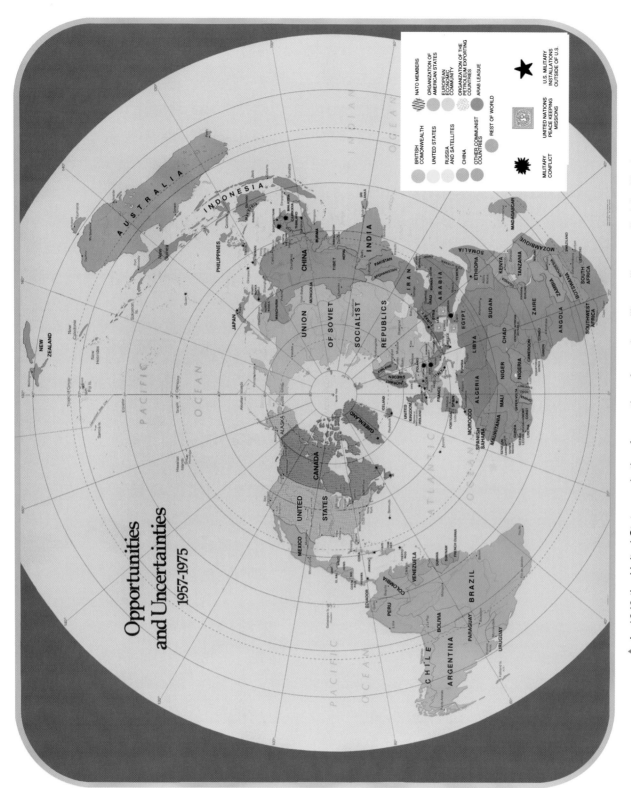

Opportunities and Uncertainties
1957-1975

▲ In 1949 the United States and other free nations formed a military alliance called the North Atlantic Treaty Organization (NATO) to prevent the spread of communism. The Soviet Union and other communist countries formed a competing alliance called the Warsaw Pact. This view indicates why Canada and the United States feared a possible Soviet attack from the north.

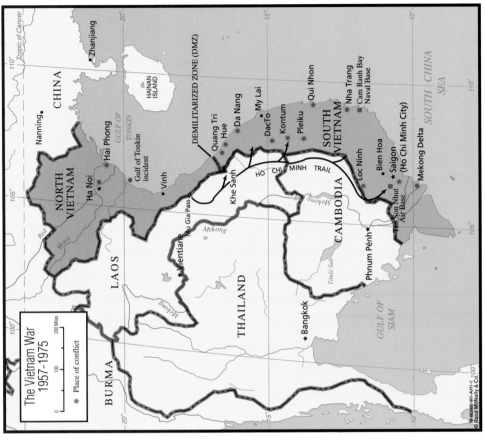

The Vietnam War 1957-1975

* Place of conflict

0   50   100   200 Miles

CHINA

Zhanjiang

Nanning

NORTH VIETNAM

Hai Phong

Ha Noi

Vinh

GULF OF TONKIN

Gulf of Tonkin incident

HAINAN ISLAND

DEMILITARIZED ZONE (DMZ)

Quang Tri
Hue
Da Nang
My Lai
DacTo
Kontum
Pleiku
Qui Nhon

Nha Trang
Cam Ranh Bay Naval Base

SOUTH CHINA SEA

Khe Sanh

Mu Gia Pass

HO CHI MINH TRAIL

SOUTH VIETNAM

Loc Ninh
Bien Hoa
Saigon (Ho Chi Minh City)
Tan Son Nhut Air Base
Mekong Delta

LAOS

Ventiane

Mekong

CAMBODIA

Phnum Pénh

Tonlé Sab

THAILAND

Bangkok

BURMA

GULF OF SIAM

Red
Black
Mekong

M-68300-9H-AH1-1
© Rand McNally & Co.

▲ The United States entered the longest war in its history to prevent communist-ruled North Vietnam from taking over non-communist South Vietnam. The Ho Chi Minh Trail was a system of roads the North Vietnamese used as a supply route for the Viet Cong, or communist rebels in South Vietnam.

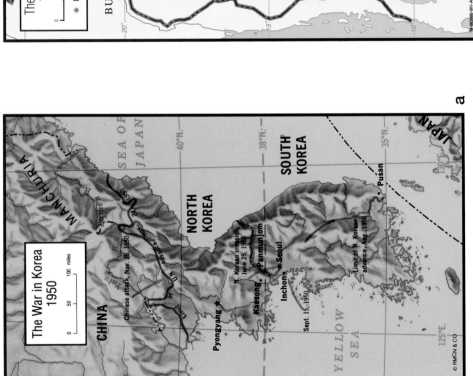

The War in Korea 1950

0   50   100 miles

CHINA

MANCHURIA

SEA OF JAPAN

Chinese attack, Nov. 26, 1950

Yalu

Limit of Chinese advance, 1950

NORTH KOREA

Pyongyang

Kaesong
Panmunjom
Inchon
Seoul
Sept. 15, 1950

N. Korean invasion, June 25, 1950

SOUTH KOREA

Limit of N. Korean advance, Aug. 1950

Pusan

YELLOW SEA

JAPAN

40°N.
38°N.
35°N.
125°E.
130°E.

© RMCN & CO

▲ United Nations members, including the United States, sent troops to defend South Korea from an invasion by communist-ruled North Korea. In 1950, UN forces halted the North Korean advance at Pusan and pushed to the Yalu River in the north. The war ended in 1953 when the UN and North Korea signed an armistice agreement.

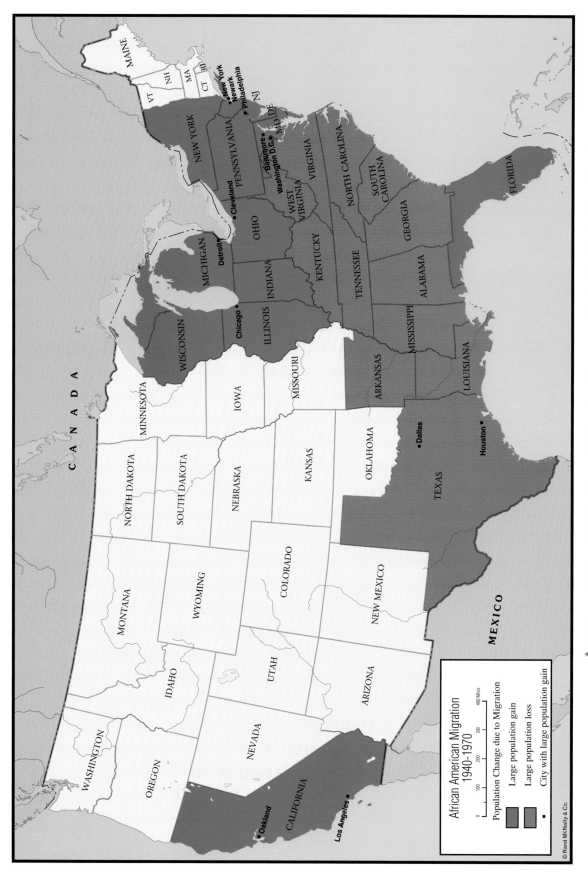

African American Migration 1940-1970

Population Change due to Migration

- Large population gain
- Large population loss
- ■ City with large population gain

0 100 200 300 400 Miles

© Rand McNally & Co.

▲ *Between 1940 and 1970, millions of African Americans moved out of the South. More than two-thirds of the total African American population relocated to cities. More than half the urban black population was concentrated in the twelve cities shown on the map.*

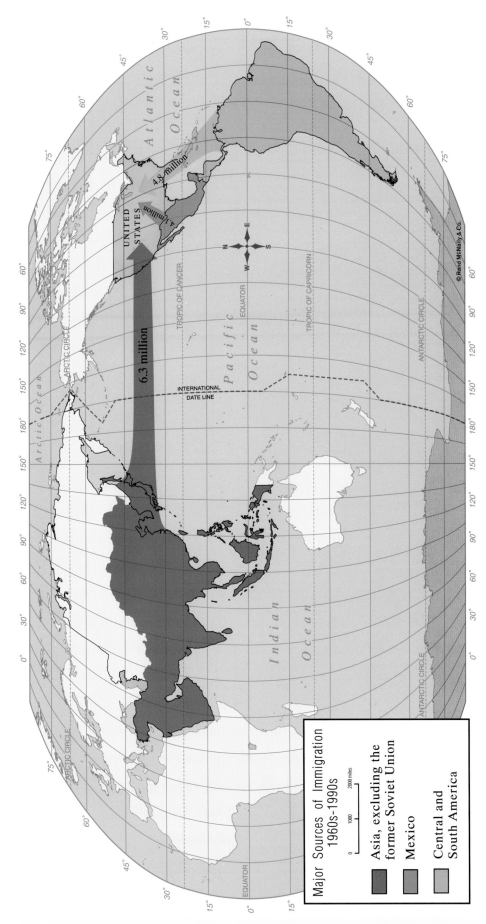

▲ Changes in U.S. immigration laws in the 1960s changed immigration patterns. Percentages of immigrants from Europe decreased. In the 1990s, most immigrants to the United States came from Mexico, the Philippines, Haiti, China, India, Vietnam, Jamaica, Cuba, and South Korea.

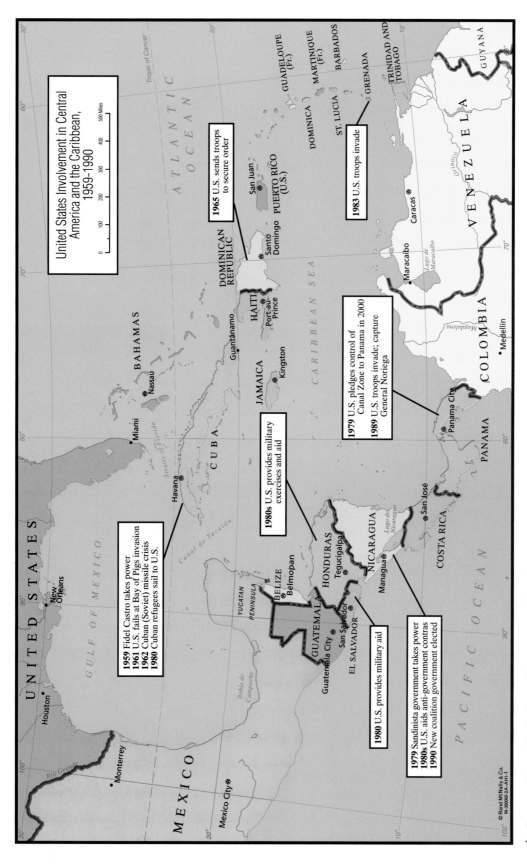

United States Involvement in Central America and the Caribbean, 1959-1990

1959 Fidel Castro takes power
1961 U.S. fails at Bay of Pigs invasion
1962 Cuban (Soviet) missile crisis
1980 Cuban refugees sail to U.S.

1965 U.S. sends troops to secure order

1983 U.S. troops invade

1979 U.S. pledges control of Canal Zone to Panama in 2000
1989 U.S. troops invade; capture General Noriega

1980s U.S. provides military exercises and aid

1980 U.S. provides military aid

1979 Sandinista government takes power
1980s U.S. aids anti-government contras
1990 New coalition government elected

© Rand McNally & Co.
M-300002-2A-AH-1

▲ *Communist activity in Central America and the Caribbean threatened U.S. security. In 1962 the Cuban missile crisis led the United States to the brink of nuclear war with the Soviet Union. The United States continued to intervene in the region to support democracy and to protect U.S. interests.*

Section 8 *(1990 & beyond)*

Entering a New Millennium

In 1990 the United States was one of the world's leading nations. Its resources and technology made it a leader in the production of goods and services. Its principles of freedom and opportunity provided its people with one of the world's highest standards of living.

The diverse population of the United States reflected the history of a nation settled by people from every part of the world. According to the 1990 census, most Americans lived throughout the country in large **metropolitan areas**, or cities surrounded by suburbs. They earned more money and lived longer than Americans in the past. In spite of widespread prosperity, however, many Americans lived in poverty.

As the United States enters a new millennium, it must consider ways to meet the needs of an aging population. It also faces challenges in a changing world. Defending human rights, supporting economic development, and protecting the environment have become global issues.

◀ *Skyscrapers tower over midtown Manhattan in New York – the largest U.S. city in population in 1990.*

Seattle, Washington, became an aerospace and technology center as well as a leading U.S. port for Pacific Rim trade. ▶

Did You Know ?

More than half the people who lived in the Los Angeles metropolitan area in 1990 moved there from other countries or other parts of the United States.

Population Distribution by Age, 1990

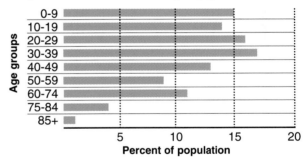

Age groups: 0-9, 10-19, 20-29, 30-39, 40-49, 50-59, 60-74, 75-84, 85+

Percent of population: 5, 10, 15, 20

	1992	1992	1997
People	Mae Carol Jemison, of Illinois, becomes first African American woman to travel in space.	Ross Perot, of Texas, runs as independent candidate for President of the United States.	Madeleine Albright, who was born in Czechoslovakia, becomes first woman U.S. secretary of state.
	1991	1992	1994
Events	Collapse of the Soviet Union marks end of Cold War.	World leaders hold Earth Summit in Rio de Janeiro, Brazil.	United States, Canada, and Mexico sign North American Free Trade Agreement (NAFTA).
	1991	1991	1993
Literature	*There Are No Children Here*, by Alex Kotlowitz, describes social conditions in Chicago's inner city.	*The Lost Garden*, by Laurence Yep, describes how the author grew up as a Chinese American in San Francisco.	*Having Our Say*, by the Delany sisters, describes 100 years of African American life in North Carolina and New York, NY.

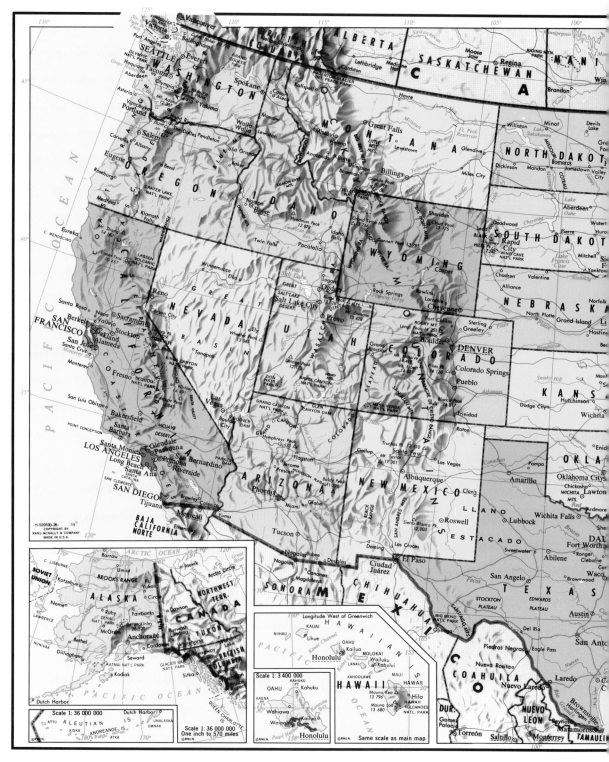

▲ *In 1990 the United States had more than 350 metropolitan areas. The largest of these areas are indicated in red on the map. Los Angeles-Long Beach had a 1990 population of almost 9 million, making it the country's largest metropolitan area in population.*

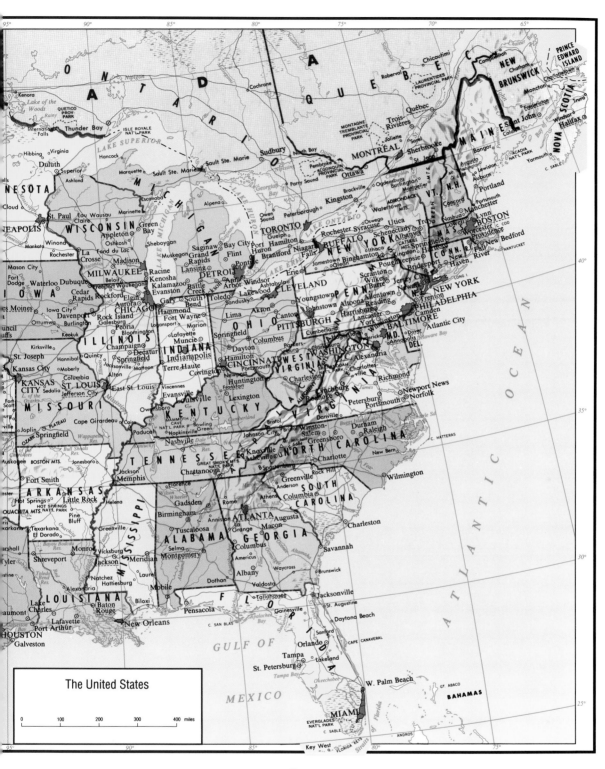

The United States

Cities and Towns

0 to 50,000	○
50,000 to 500,000	⊙
500,000 to 1,000,000	◎
1,000,000 and over	⬤

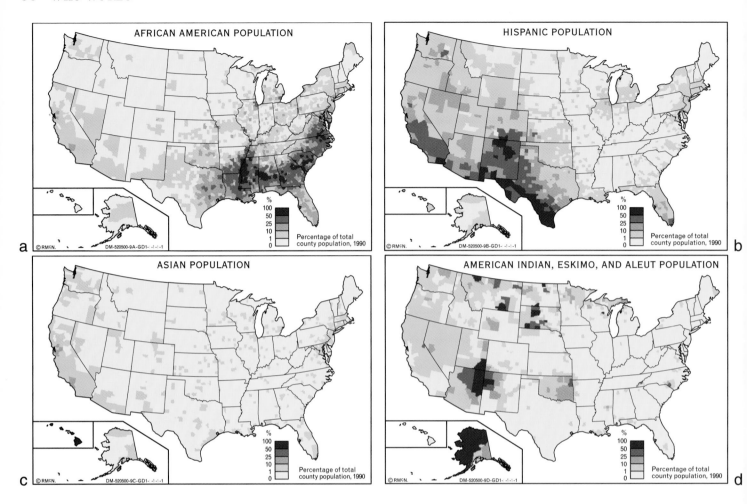

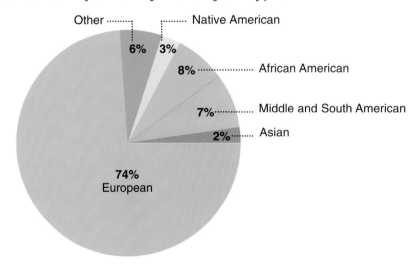

United States Population by Ancestry Group, 1990

Other — 6%

Native American — 3%

African American — 8%

Middle and South American — 7%

Asian — 2%

74% European

The maps show some major racial/ethnic groups in the United States in 1990 and where they lived. The graph shows the percentages of people of different ancestry groups within the United States population in 1990.

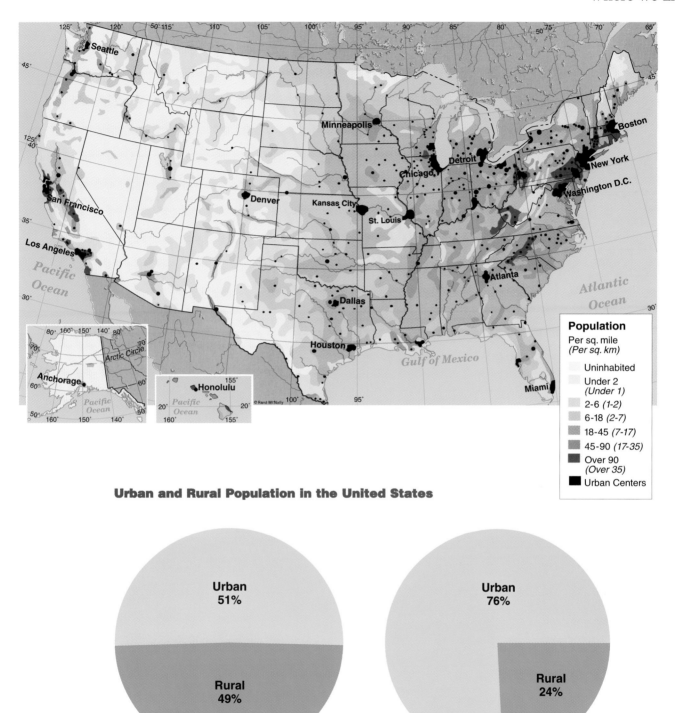

Urban and Rural Population in the United States

1920s
- Urban 51%
- Rural 49%

1990s
- Urban 76%
- Rural 24%

In 1990 more than three-fourths of all Americans lived in urban areas. The map shows the locations of the most densely populated parts of the United States. Notice that several metropolitan areas from Boston to Washington, D.C. had grown together to form a large, densely populated area called a megalopolis. The circle graphs compare the percentages of urban and rural population in the United States in the 1920s and 1990s.

Median Family Income, 1990

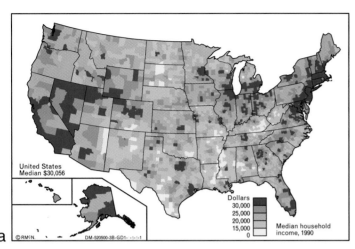

United States
Median $30,056

Dollars
30,000
25,000
20,000
15,000
0

Median household
income, 1990

a ©RM°N. DM-520500-3B-GD1- -1-1-1

▲ *The map shows median family income, or
the middle value of all family incomes, in
different parts of the United States in
1990.*

Lifetime Expectance, 1990

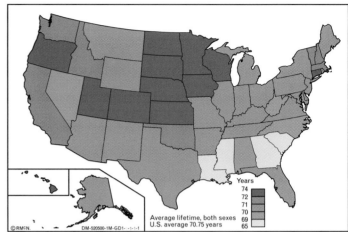

Years
74
72
71
70
69
65

Average lifetime, both sexes
U.S. average 70.75 years

©RM°N. DM-520500-1M-GD1- -1-1-1

▲ *The map shows the average lifetime of all
Americans in different parts of the United
States in 1990.*

Median Family Income
(in current dollars), 1960-1990

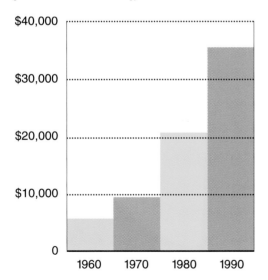

▲ *The graph shows how median family
income throughout the United States
changed between 1960 and 1990.*

Lifetime Expectance of Males and Females
1900-1990

	Year of Birth	
Male - years		**Female - years**
46	**1900**	48
48	**1910**	52
54	**1920**	55
58	**1930**	62
61	**1940**	65
66	**1950**	71
67	**1960**	73
67	**1970**	75
70	**1980**	77
72	**1990**	79

▲ *The graph shows how average lifetimes of
males and females in the United States
changed between 1900 and 1990.*

Percentage of U.S. Population Below Poverty Level, 1990

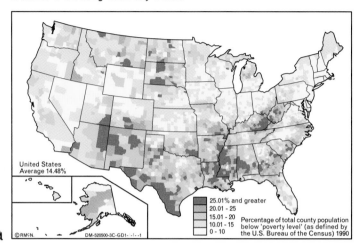

United States Average 14.48%

25.01% and greater
20.01 - 25
15.01 - 20
10.01 - 15
0 - 10

Percentage of total county population below 'poverty level' (as defined by the U.S. Bureau of the Census) 1990

©RM&N.   DM-520500-3C-GD1- -:- -1

▲ The map shows the percentages of people living below the poverty level in different parts of the United States in 1990. Poverty level is based on the income needed to feed a family adequately without spending more than a third of the family income on food.

U.S. Unemployment Rates, 1990

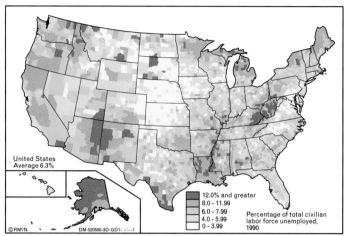

United States Average 6.3%

12.0% and greater
8.0 - 11.99
6.0 - 7.99
4.0 - 5.99
0 - 3.99

Percentage of total civilian labor force unemployed, 1990

©RM&N.   DM-520500-3D-GD1- -:- -1   b

▲ The map shows the percentages of unemployed workers in different parts of the United States in 1990.

Percentage of U.S. Population Below Poverty Level, 1960-1990

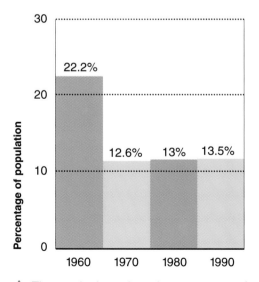

Percentage of population

22.2%   12.6%   13%   13.5%
1960   1970   1980   1990

▲ The graph shows how the percentage of Americans below the poverty level changed between 1960 and 1990.

U.S. Unemployment Rates, 1960-1990

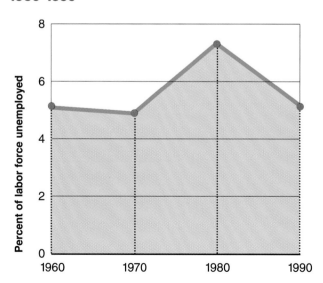

Percent of labor force unemployed

1960   1970   1980   1990

▲ The graph shows how the percentage of unemployed workers in the United States changed between 1960 and 1990.

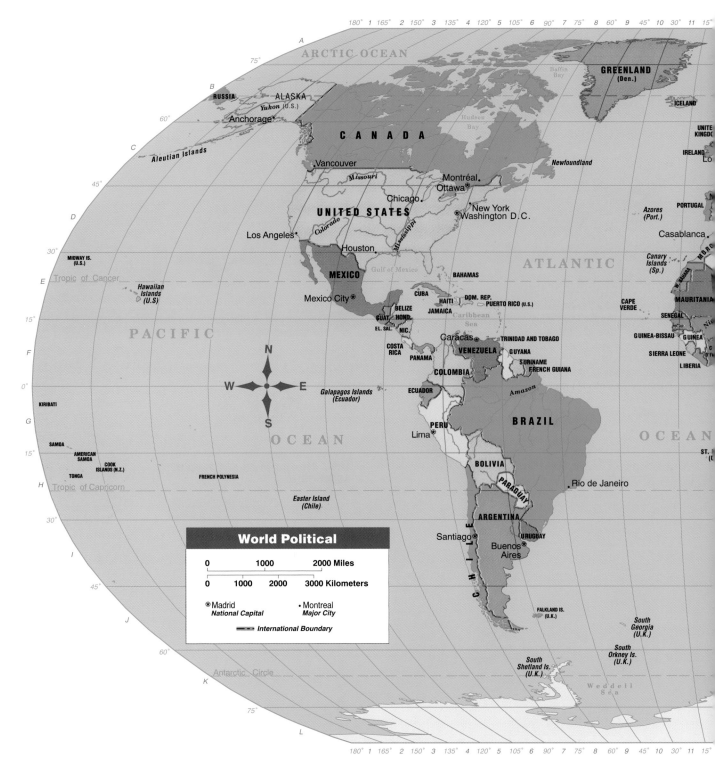

The 50 states that make up the United States cover an area of more than 3 1/2 million square miles. The United States is the world's fourth largest country in area.

In 1990 the United States had a population of about 250 million. It was the world's third largest country in population.

Populations of United States Colonies and States, 1650-1990

States	1650	1700	1750	1770	1790	1800	1820	1840
Alabama							127,901	590,756
Alaska								
Arizona								
Arkansas							14,273	97,574
California								
Colorado								
Connecticut	4,139	25,970	111,280	183,881	237,946	251,002	275,248	309,978
Delaware	185	2,470	28,704	35,496	59,096	64,273	72,749	78,085
District of Columbia						8,144	23,336	33,745
Florida								54,477
Georgia			5,200	23,375	82,548	162,686	340,989	691,392
Hawaii								
Idaho								
Illinois							55,211	476,183
Indiana						5,641	147,178	685,866
Iowa								43,112
Kansas								
Kentucky				15,700	73,677	220,955	564,317	779,828
Louisiana							153,407	352,411
Maine[4]				31,257	96,540	151,719	298,335	501,793
Maryland	4,504	29,604	141,073	202,599	319,728	341,548	407,350	470,019
Massachusetts[4]	16,603	55,941	188,000	235,308	378,787	422,845	523,287	737,699
Michigan							8,896	212,267
Minnesota								
Mississippi						8,850	75,448	375,651
Missouri							66,586	383,702
Montana								
Nebraska								
Nevada								
New Hampshire	1,305	4,958	27,505	62,396	141,885	183,858	244,161	284,574
New Jersey		14,010	71,393	117,431	184,139	211,149	277,575	373,306
New Mexico								
New York	4,116	19,107	76,696	162,920	340,120	589,051	1,372,812	2,428,921
North Carolina		10,720	72,984	197,200	393,751	478,103	638,829	753,419
North Dakota[3]								
Ohio						45,365	581,434	1,519,467
Oklahoma[5]								
Oregon								
Pennsylvania		17,950	119,666	240,057	434,373	602,365	1,049,458	1,724,033
Rhode Island	785	5,894	33,226	58,196	68,825	69,122	83,059	108,830
South Carolina		5,704	64,000	124,244	249,073	345,591	502,741	594,398
South Dakota[3]								
Tennessee				1,000	35,691	105,602	422,823	829,210
Texas								
Utah								
Vermont				10,000	85,425	154,465	235,981	291,948
Virginia[6]	18,731	58,560	231,033	447,016	691,737	807,557	938,261	1,025,227
Washington								
West Virginia[6]					55,873	78,592	136,808	224,537
Wisconsin								30,945
Wyoming								
Total[1]	50,368	250,888	1,170,760	2,148,076	3,929,214	5,308,483	9,638,453	17,069,453[2]

[1] All figures prior to 1890 exclude Indians unaffected by the pioneer movement. Figures for 1650 through 1770 include only the British colonies that later became the United States. No areas are included prior to their annexation to the United States. However, many of the figures refer to territories prior to their admission as states. U.S. total includes Alaska from 1880 through 1970 and Hawaii from 1900 through 1970.

[2] U.S. total for 1840 includes 6,100 persons on public ships in service of the United States not credited to any state.

[3] South Dakota figure for 1860 represents entire Dakota Territory. North and South Dakota figures for 1880 are for the parts of Dakota Territory which later constituted the respective states.

1860	1880	1900	1920	1940	1950	1960	1970	1980	1990
964,201	1,262,505	1,828,697	2,348,174	2,832,961	3,061,743	3,266,740	3,444,165	3,893,888	4,062,608
	33,426	63,592	55,036	72,524	128,643	226,167	302,173	401,851	551,947
	40,440	122,931	334,162	499,261	749,587	1,302,161	1,772,482	2,718,425	3,677,985
435,450	802,525	1,311,564	1,752,204	1,949,387	1,909,511	1,786,272	1,923,295	2,286,435	2,362,239
379,994	864,694	1,485,053	3,426,861	6,907,387	10,586,223	15,717,204	19,953,134	23,667,565	29,839,250
34,277	194,327	539,700	939,629	1,123,296	1,325,089	1,753,947	2,207,259	2,889,735	3,307,912
460,147	622,700	908,420	1,380,631	1,709,242	2,007,280	2,535,234	3,032,217	3,107,576	3,295,669
112,216	146,608	184,735	223,003	266,505	318,085	446,292	548,104	594,317	668,696
75,080	177,624	278,718	437,571	663,091	802,178	763,956	756,510	638,432	609,909
140,424	269,493	528,542	968,470	1,897,414	2,771,305	4,951,560	6,789,443	9,746,342	13,003,362
1,057,286	1,542,180	2,216,331	2,895,832	3,123,723	3,444,578	3,943,116	4,589,575	5,463,105	6,508,419
		154,001	255,881	422,770	499,794	632,772	769,913	964,691	1,115,274
	32,610	161,772	431,866	524,873	588,637	667,191	713,008	944,038	1,011,986
1,711,951	3,077,871	4,821,550	6,485,280	7,897,241	8,712,176	10,081,158	11,113,976	11,426,596	11,466,682
1,350,428	1,978,301	2,516,462	2,930,390	3,427,796	3,934,224	4,662,498	5,193,669	5,490,260	5,564,228
674,913	1,624,615	2,231,853	2,404,021	2,538,268	2,621,073	2,757,537	2,825,041	2,913,808	2,787,424
107,206	996,096	1,470,495	1,769,257	1,801,028	1,905,299	2,178,611	2,249,071	2,364,236	2,485,600
1,155,684	1,648,690	2,147,174	2,416,630	2,845,627	2,944,806	3,038,156	3,219,311	3,660,257	3,698,969
708,002	939,946	1,381,625	1,798,509	2,363,880	2,683,516	3,257,022	3,643,180	4,206,312	4,238,216
628,279	648,936	694,466	768,014	847,226	913,774	969,265	993,663	1,125,027	1,233,223
687,049	934,943	1,188,044	1,449,661	1,821,244	2,343,001	3,100,689	3,922,399	4,216,975	4,798,622
1,231,066	1,783,085	2,805,346	3,852,356	4,316,721	4,690,514	5,148,578	5,689,170	5,737,037	6,029,051
749,113	1,636,937	2,420,982	3,668,412	5,256,106	6,371,766	7,823,194	8,875,083	9,262,078	9,328,784
172,023	780,773	1,751,394	2,387,125	2,792,300	2,982,483	3,413,864	3,805,069	4,075,970	4,387,029
791,305	1,131,597	1,551,270	1,790,618	2,183,796	2,178,914	2,178,141	2,216,912	2,520,638	2,586,443
1,182,012	2,168,380	3,106,665	3,404,055	3,784,664	3,954,653	4,319,813	4,677,399	4,916,759	5,137,804
	39,159	243,329	548,889	559,456	591,024	674,767	694,409	786,690	803,655
28,841	452,402	1,066,300	1,296,372	1,315,834	1,325,510	1,411,330	1,483,791	1,569,825	1,584,617
6,857	62,266	42,335	77,407	110,247	160,083	285,278	488,738	800,493	1,206,152
326,073	346,991	411,488	443,083	491,524	533,242	606,921	737,681	920,610	1,113,915
672,035	1,131,116	1,883,669	3,155,900	4,160,165	4,835,329	6,066,782	7,168,164	7,364,823	7,748,634
93,516	119,565	195,310	360,350	531,818	681,187	951,023	1,016,000	1,302,981	1,521,779
3,880,735	5,082,871	7,268,894	10,385,227	13,479,142	14,830,192	16,782,304	18,241,266	17,558,072	18,044,505
992,622	1,399,750	1,893,810	2,559,123	3,571,623	4,061,929	4,556,155	5,082,059	5,881,813	6,657,630
	36,909	319,146	646,872	641,935	619,636	632,446	617,761	652,717	641,364
2,339,511	3,198,062	4,157,545	5,759,394	6,907,612	7,946,627	9,706,397	10,652,017	10,797,624	10,887,325
		790,391	2,028,283	2,336,434	2,233,351	2,328,284	2,559,253	3,025,290	3,157,604
52,465	174,768	413,536	783,389	1,089,684	1,521,341	1,768,687	2,091,385	2,633,149	2,853,733
2,906,215	4,282,891	6,302,115	8,720,017	9,900,180	10,498,012	11,319,366	11,793,909	11,863,895	11,924,710
174,620	276,531	428,556	604,397	713,346	791,896	859,488	949,723	947,154	1,005,984
703,708	995,577	1,340,316	1,683,724	1,899,804	2,117,027	2,382,594	2,590,516	3,121,833	3,505,707
4,837	98,268	401,570	636,547	642,961	652,740	680,514	666,257	690,768	699,999
1,109,801	1,542,359	2,020,616	2,337,885	2,915,841	3,291,718	3,567,089	3,924,164	4,591,120	4,896,641
604,215	1,591,749	3,048,710	4,663,228	6,414,824	7,711,194	9,579,677	11,196,730	14,229,288	17,059,805
40,273	143,963	276,749	449,396	550,310	688,862	890,627	1,059,273	1,461,037	1,727,784
315,098	332,286	343,641	352,428	359,231	377,747	389,881	444,732	551,456	564,964
1,219,630	1,512,565	1,854,184	2,309,187	2,677,773	3,318,680	3,966,949	4,648,494	5,346,818	6,216,568
11,594	75,116	518,103	1,356,621	1,736,191	2,378,963	2,853,214	3,409,169	4,132,180	4,887,941
376,688	618,457	958,800	1,463,701	1,901,974	2,005,552	1,860,421	1,744,237	1,950,279	1,801,625
775,881	1,315,497	2,069,042	2,632,067	3,137,587	3,434,575	3,951,777	4,417,933	4,705,521	4,906,745
	20,789	92,531	194,402	250,742	290,529	330,066	332,416	469,557	455,975
31,443,321	**50,189,209**	**76,212,168**	**106,021,537**	**132,164,569**	**151,325,798**	**179,323,175**	**203,235,298**	**226,547,346**	**249,632,692**

[4]Maine figures for 1770 through 1800 are for that area of Massachusetts which became the state of Maine in 1820. Massachusetts figures exclude Maine from 1770 through 1800, but include it from 1650 through 1750. Massachusetts figure for 1650 also includes population of Plymouth (1,566), a separate colony until 1691.

[5]Oklahoma figure for 1900 includes population of Indian Territory (392,060).

[6]West Virginia figures for 1790 through 1860 are for that area of Virginia which became West Virginia in 1863. These figures are excluded from the figures for Virginia from 1790 through 1860.

Facts About the States

State	Admission to the Union date (order)	Capital	Area in sq.mi. (rank in area)	Nickname	Postal Abbreviation
Alabama	1819 (22)	Montgomery	51,705 (29)	The Heart of Dixie	AL
Alaska	1959 (49)	Juneau	591,004 (1)	Last Frontier	AK
Arizona	1912 (48)	Phoenix	114,000 (6)	Grand Canyon State	AZ
Arkansas	1836 (25)	Little Rock	53,187 (27)	Land of Opportunity	AR
California	1850 (31)	Sacramento	158,706 (3)	Golden State	CA
Colorado	1876 (38)	Denver	104,091 (8)	Centennial State	CO
Connecticut	1788 (5)	Hartford	5.018 (48)	Constitution State	CT
Delaware	1787 (1)	Dover	2,044 (49)	First State	DE
Florida	1845 (27)	Tallahassee	58,664 (22)	Sunshine State	FL
Georgia	1788 (4)	Atlanta	58,910 (21)	Empire State of the South	GA
Hawaii	1959 (50)	Honolulu	6,471 (47)	Aloha State	HI
Idaho	1890 (43)	Boise	83,564 (13)	Gem State	ID
Illinois	1818 (21)	Springfield	56,345 (24)	Land of Lincoln	IL
Indiana	1816 (19)	Indianapolis	36,185 (38)	Hoosier State	IN
Iowa	1846 (29)	Des Moines	56,275 (25)	Hawkeye State	IA
Kansas	1861 (34)	Topeka	82,277 (14)	Sunflower State	KS
Kentucky	1792 (15)	Frankfort	40,409 (37)	Bluegrass State	KY
Louisiana	1812 (18)	Baton Rouge	47,752 (31)	Pelican State	LA
Maine	1820 (23)	Augusta	33,265 (39)	Pine Tree State	ME
Maryland	1788 (7)	Annapolis	10,460 (42)	Old Line State	MD
Massachusetts	1788 (6)	Boston	8,284 (45)	Bay State	MA
Michigan	1837 (26)	Lansing	58,527 (23)	Wolverine State	MI
Minnesota	1858 (32)	St. Paul	84,402 (12)	Gopher State	MN
Mississippi	1817 (20)	Jackson	47,689 (32)	Magnolia State	MS
Missouri	1821 (24)	Jefferson City	69,697 (19)	Show Me State	MO

State	Admission to the Union date (order)	Capital	Area in sq.mi. (rank in area)	Nickname	Postal Abbreviation
Montana	1889 (41)	Helena	147,046 (4)	Treasure State	MT
Nebraska	1867 (37)	Lincoln	77,355 (15)	Cornhusker State	NE
Nevada	1864 (36)	Carson City	110,561 (7)	Silver State	NV
New Hampshire	1788 (9)	Concord	9,297 (44)	Granite State	NH
New Jersey	1787 (3)	Trenton	7,787 (46)	Garden State	NJ
New Mexico	1912 (47)	Santa Fe	121,593 (5)	Land of Enchantment	NM
New York	1788 (11)	Albany	49,108 (30)	Empire State	NY
North Carolina	1789 (12)	Raleigh	52,669 (28)	Tar Heel State	NC
North Dakota	1889 (39)	Bismarck	70,702 (17)	Flickertail State	ND
Ohio	1803 (17)	Columbus	41,330 (35)	Buckeye State	OH
Oklahoma	1907 (46)	Oklahoma City	69,956 (18)	Sooner State	OK
Oregon	1859 (33)	Salem	97,073 (10)	Beaver State	OR
Pennsylvania	1787 (2)	Harrisburg	45,308 (33)	Keystone State	PA
Rhode Island	1790 (13)	Providence	1,212 (50)	Ocean State	RI
South Carolina	1788 (8)	Columbia	31,113 (40)	Palmetto State	SC
South Dakota	1889 (40)	Pierre	77,116 (16)	Mount Rushmore State	SD
Tennessee	1796 (16)	Nashville	42,114 (34)	Volunteer State	TN
Texas	1845 (28)	Austin	266,807 (2)	Lone Star State	TX
Utah	1896 (45)	Salt Lake City	84,899 (11)	Beehive State	UT
Vermont	1791 (14)	Montpelier	9,614 (43)	Green Mountain State	VT
Virginia	1788 (10)	Richmond	40,767 (36)	Old Dominion	VA
Washington	1889 (42)	Olympia	68,139 (20)	Evergreen State	WA
West Virginia	1863 (35)	Charleston	24,231 (41)	Mountain State	WV
Wisconsin	1848 (30)	Madison	56,153 (26)	Badger State	WI
Wyoming	1890 (44)	Cheyenne	97,809 (9)	Equality State	WY

In addition to place names that appear on the maps in this atlas, the Index also lists names of people, groups, events, and other topics related to American history. It provides explanatory information, such as dates, identifications, and geographic locations for many entries. When appropriate, entries are cross-referenced to related topics.

The Index lists boldfaced page numbers on which each entry appears. A small letter beside a page number identifies a specific map on the page on which the entry appears. Postal abbreviations are used for state names.

The following abbreviations also are used:

Ft.   Fort   St.   Saint
g   graph   t   table
Is.   Islands   terr. territory
p   photograph   U.S.   United States
pop.   population